Critical Acclaim for

Shaking Out the Spirits

Bradford Keeney walks us right into the maze of the human spirit. His portraits of elder healers and trans-global visionaries light up the dark horizon at the end of this century. Reading his account of the shamanic journey, I felt like the universe dreamed him up to doctor its own misguided soul. His book will shake and rattle its way into your heart.

Nor Hall, PH.D., author of *The Moon and the Virgin* and *Those Women*

If *The Celestine Prophecy* opened your eyes and excited your mind with a vision of new realms of experiences, hear the good news: *Shaking Out the Spirits* offers you a personal journey in the company of a man who lives that vision.

Julie Henderson, PH.D., author, *The Lover Within*

This is a gripping account of an almost incredible journey that Keeney, a prolific author, professor, and psychotherapist, took into shamanism as practiced in remote areas of several continents.

Library Journal

This unique shamanic journey is a guide into the holy centers of diverse spiritual traditions throughout the world. Bringing non-ordinary reality, miraculous discovery, and mysteries to the reader, Bradford Keeney's story voices the personal heart and power of healing love. If the human race is to avoid self-destruction, this song of shared spiritual harmony must be learned.

Cynthia Bend, coauthor, *Birth of a Modern Shaman*

A remarkable book in its courage, integrity, and promise that embraces all religions, all traditions.

The Phoenix

Black Elk

Shaking Out the Spirits

A Psychotherapist's Entry into the
Healing Mysteries of Global Shamanism

Bradford Keeney

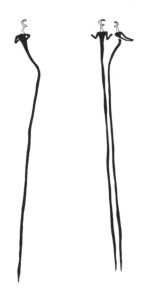

Foreword by Stephen Larsen

Station Hill Press

Published by Station Hill Press, Inc., Barrytown, New York, 12507.

Text and cover design by Susan Quasha, assisted by Vicki Hickman.

Photograph of Black Elk (frontispiece) courtesy of the National Anthropological Archives, Smithsonian Institution.

Library of Congress Cataloging-in-Publication Data

Keeney, Bradford P.
  Shaking out the spirits : a psychologist's entry into the healing mysteries
  of global shamanism / Bradford Powell Keeney.
      p. cm.
  ISBN 0-88268-164-8 : $13.95
  1. Shamanism. 2. Mental healing. 3. Indians of North America—Religion and
mythology. 4. Keeney, Bradford P. I. Title.
  BF1611.K33 1994
  291.1'4—dc20   93-48357
                                                        CIP

Manufactured in the United States of America.

Dedicated to
my wife, Marian
and
my son, Scott

Of course it was not I who cured. It was the power from the outer world, and the visions and ceremonies had only made me like a hole through which the power would come to the two-leggeds. If I thought that I was doing it myself, the hole would close up and no power would come through it.

Black Elk

Re-examine all you have been told at school or church or in any book, dismiss whatever insults your own soul, and your very flesh shall be a great poem and have the richest fluency not only in its words, but in the silent lines of its lips and face and between the lashes of your eyes and in every motion and joint of your body.

Walt Whitman

Contents

Photographs

Foreword

Stephen Larsen

This is a book that the genuine spiritual seeker may have trouble putting down. If you're like me, you will feel your very life-force electrified; your spine will tingle, your ears will flush, and your eyes will become bright with dew as you follow Bradford Keeney through his amazing spirit-filled adventures. Please fasten your seat belts.

Some of us first encountered this feeling reading Castaneda. It did not matter much to us whether it was ethnography or myth we were reading. Those luminous supernatural beings in that desert landscape — giant spirit moths, the vegetal ally Mescalito, the sorceror's tentacles that hold Don Genaro to the slippery rocks at the top of the vertiginous waterfall — all were instantly a part of our mindscapes. We were waiting for them as if we needed them, somehow. They broke through into our personal mythologies.

Centuries ago, now, it seems, the bright images of the Olympians, the Nordic and Celtic gods, the fey hosts of the Sidhe and the Wild Hunt, quit the mythic stage, leaving a vacancy, an arid wasteland in the soul. And the Great Goddess with her life-bestowing bounty left not centuries, but millennia ago. Recently, Church calendars and newsletters try ever more desperately to refute Nietzsche's ringing "God is dead." We seem to be left, nay abandoned, in a vast mindless universe of hurrying matter —"alone and afraid in a world we never made. . . ."

Once, in a moment of unusual clarity and insight, I saw what a truly odd mix I was: a demythologized, skeptical, half crazed, yet spiritually thirsty creature. In college, like many of us, I had lost the religion of my childhood to secular scientism. Thereafter I went through an awful period of being lost and depressed. Life seemed to have no intrinsic meaning aside from economic and social struggle. I saw myself to be naked and frightened in a boundless metaphysical void. I was condescending to, even while envying, those of my contemporaries who had managed to cling to a faith of some sort throughout the storms of psychospiritual adolescence — they at least enjoyed the shelter of mythological umbrellas.

In the early sixties, a book, relatively obscure at that time, restored me to some sense of spiritual context for my life. The book was Joseph Campbell's *The Hero with a Thousand Faces*. It was not a recognizeably spiritual text, and yet it suggested that interlaced through all of the world's great mythological traditions was a sense of the sacred journey of life's becoming. It effected in me a spiritual awakening. I found myself to be back on the path, but exactly what path, (as I romanced through Jungian archetypes, the I Ching, the Eastern disciplines), I had yet to discover.

Then I found shamanism, and for the first time understood the significance of my own psychological dismemberment. Shamanism for me was the beginning of the journey, the call to adventure — and it was also like a primordial homecoming. Could it be that from the beginning of time, broken men and women have dipped into something called "the sacred" and been restored? Wouldn't it still be present, if we only knew how to find it? Can't the spirits still sing and drum their immemorial spirit songs into our souls? I joined a generation hungry for inspiration, and some of us leaped straight from Castaneda into the dusty pages of anthropological journals.

In writing *The Shaman's Doorway* in 1974-5, I hoped somehow to share a vision, to re-introduce the world of magic and spiritual possibility to contemporary seekers, people as desperate for meaning as I was. (At the time all that was popularly available on the subject was the work of Eliade, rich and comprehensive, but dry.) Now, twenty years later, there are dozens of books on shamanism, several worldwide societies to further scholarly shamanic studies, and an excellent journal for the layman, *The Shaman's Drum*. Long untraveled, the spirit way of the old ones seems determined to open in our lives. As the millenium approaches, it as though the spirit world were cracklingly alive with dreams, visions and transformations. And people are looking everywhere for guidance in the encounter with that world of living forces. *Shaking Out The Spirits* offers an important source of that guidance.

It would have been useful years ago to have such a book. As I sat down in my little house in the woods to write about the great Oglala Sioux Holy Man, Black Elk, I had my own experience of "vibration." Powerful currents moved up and down my spine and tears ran down my cheeks as I relived the luminous visions of that solitary nine-year old Indian boy. I wept for him and the plight of his people. The power of his vision filled my heart till I thought it would break, as I sensed what that vision must have meant to his dying nation, leading them, as it did, to a great healing enactment. Black Elk said:

> Then suddenly as I sat there looking at the cloud, I saw my vision yonder once again — the tepee built of cloud and sewed with lightning, the flaming rainbow door and underneath, the six grandfather's sitting, and also there was I myself upon my bay before the tepee. I looked about me and could see that what we then were doing was like a shadow cast upon the earth from

yonder vision in the heavens, so bright it was and clear. I knew the real was yonder and the darkened dream of it was here. (Neihardt, *Black Elk Speaks*, pp 173-74).

Those lines have been ringing in my mind ever since: "The real was yonder, and the darkened dream of it was here." Is there in truth not a world of greater caring, knowing and creativity parallel to our own? And is participation in that world not the most meaningful experience available to us? It may at all events be our last only chance to find the unity in our broken, suffering world.

Black Elk knew his vision was meant to heal his own people, but it also concerned a larger destiny: "And I saw that the sacred hoop of my own people was one of many hoops that made one circle, wide as daylight and as starlight, and in the center grew one mighty flowering tree to shelter all the children of one mother and one father. And I saw that it was holy." (*Black Elk Speaks*, p.43)

And so it was that Bradford Keeney's own great vision began near a library where, unknown to him at the time, Neihardt's notes of his conversations with Black Elk were stored, setting him off on the series of adventures chronicled in this book. The author was to travel full circle before he fully realized the presence and power of Black Elk and the Great Sacred Circle of many hoops.

It is this larger circle, "wide as daylight and starlight," that is being addressed through Bradford Keeney's remarkable journey, and this book that is its chronicle. Spirit has put us on notice: our world is in a time of crisis in which all races and cultures need to open their minds and hearts to each other. "There are no more boundaries," said Joseph Campbell, "We are in a free-fall into globalism." What the great scholar-visionary meant was that our sense of the sacred must detach from bondage to a specific body of mythological forms — these are only the shells of spirit — but open ever outward into an irrefutable knowledge of our common humanity and our mutual participation in a spiritual universe.

"Followers of Jesus need to rediscover how to learn from sacred places in the wild, to sweat with the breath of God's sacred stones, to fast and cry for visions. . ." writes Keeney in this spirit:

These old ways can be taught to us from other spiritual cultures. We must find out how to respect and learn from one another's visions and prayers. The coming together of the four colors of people to make a prayer is also a metaphor for how we must learn to learn from one another. (*Shaking Out the Spirits*, p. 56.)[1]

Therefore I salute this concise and luminous book of Bradford Keeney's as a major document of spiritual witness for our time. It ranks with *The Gospel of Sri Ramakrishna*, and *The Autobiography of a Yogi* in terms of the sheer revelatory power of its encounter with the sacred. Among contemporary Westerners who have experienced mystery so intimately, only Ram Dass and his association with his Indian guru (Neem Karoli Baba), seems comparable.

Keeney relates an intricate network of stories just as they happened to him, beginning with his early vision outside the library and continuing through encounters with sacred teachers in North, South and Central America, in Africa, and finally in Japan. Following the songlines, the web of destiny, the way of wyrd, he is led, on a truly sacred pilgrimage, from place to place and from encounter to encounter with spiritual power and the human beings who are gateways to this power. The cultural vessels, the trappings are different, but the message is the same: "Trust . . . open . . . pray . . . love!" Keeney finds he is becoming "just a hollow vessel" in which the spirit can move, and as it moves it shakes him and all those he touches. If you are open to its movements, it will shake you too.

"Sometimes I wonder if those spirits know what they're doing," an old Indian told J.B., who underwent a spontaneous shamanic initiation in the Canadian wilderness. "All these good Indians there and you the one that gets called" (*The Shaman's Doorway*, p. 189). Bradford Keeney may have wondered the same, a few times, as he was seized from his stable life as a university professor into a world of strange encounters with spirit, synchronicities and initiations. But the book itself manifests a sacred wholeness that unifies these seemingly fragmentary encounters.

On the New York Thruway today, I had the thought, "Do the spirits know what they're doing?" Then I began to visualize this world from the viewpoint of the spirit. Here we are, mired not only in mammalian biological reality, but social, political and economic exigencies of all kinds. We are most often, bluntly, obtuse and opaque to the world of spirit. Only at night, when we enter the floating Taoism of the REM state, are we amenable to spiritual currents, and so often it seems that, as our outer lives become more bleak, desperate, frenzied, and repressed, our dreams come alive with visions. During our waking reality we seem to need a crisis to awaken us to the world of spirit.

But in our spiritual blindness, we are also simultaneously destroying the world of nature and the spiritual realities of a thousand traditional peoples as the hegemony of technocracy sweeps their — and our — lives towards a dizzy and unknown future. Almost all mystical and apocalyptic texts seem to hint we need to be "shaken up" somehow. Now I have some personal experience of how earthquakes feel, having ridden out the San Francisco quake of '89, and they shake us up indeed, frighten us into a momentary receptivity to spirit, as we realize the fragility of all that we take so seriously most of the time.

As I continued my drive down the Thruway, I suddenly snapped out of my reverie for a moment — a huge billboard across the Thruway said "SPIRIT" in big block letters, that word alone! (It doesn't matter that it was advertising a clothing shop in Woodstock; I got the point.) If we only look sidelong, through the cracks in the visible world, we may glimpse the movements of spirit behind the scenes — in the little chance encounters, the meetings with people in meaningful ways, in lovemaking, in music and in art, and indeed whenever we are most vibrant with the energy that surges within our physical bodies and guarantees our vitality. The spirits would open us, if we would let them, to both our danger and our wondrous possibilities. We all need to "shake out the spirits."

Spirit chose Bradford Keeney because he was willing to be led, and to open himself. In so doing, he showed us that not only can nontribal people practice shamanism, they can do it with power and integrity. His journey ties together the four great nations that the Hopis and Black Elk saw must be united by spiritual channels: the black, the red, the yellow, and the white.

The symbols that emerge in his visions and experiences are what we would call "syncretic": circles, crosses, eagles, serpents, wounded Saviors — they cross cultural boundaries and derive from a deeper vocabulary of the spirit. They cause profound responses in a psyche open to their influence.

Keeney's prose, lean and clean enough to begin with, becomes incantatory, visionary, power-filled as the book progresses:

> I dreamed of how I previously had seen God as being pure light and energy. Now I was shown how this light may be transformed into any form, making it possible for all people to have an encounter with the God force. . . . When a human being sees a form of spirit, whether it be Christ, Buddha, a spirit eagle or snake, the form is a creation brought about by the interaction of a specific tradition with the unformed energy. In this way, all traditional images, spirits, and practices are one. They all belong to the great ocean of one light. (*Shaking Out the Spirits*, p. 148)

As he concludes, it is as if the mystery itself were speaking and teaching us how to approach it:

The rebirth of being in nothingness [humility] makes all spiritual gifts possible. In this middle spot of the cross of opposites, the energy of life and death may move as freely as the leaves blowing with the wind. Here the natural world enters, not the world of decaying garbage. The winged ones, the green ones, the four-leggeds, mountains, streams, and clouds may fill this emptiness. In this way the outer natural world fills the space of one's inner world. Dreams are the guide to this new way of filling the internal emptiness. What one is shown or told in dream must be found in the natural world. When it is found, the outer and inner become one. In this way our inner ecology unites with the outer ecology making the distinction between the two impossible. When this takes place we move toward a oneness with the whole natural world. We become all of our relatives. Knowing that the inside is one with the outside enables us to be in the outside with complete awareness. In this way we surrender our limited mind to become a part of a Greater Mind. This Greater Mind becomes the mind of healing. (*Shaking Out the Spirits*, pp.163-164).

Over the next period of our lives and even for generations to come, these words can be held in our hearts and minds. I invite you to live them, even a little, in your life, and your rewards will be great. May you become renewed with the deepest dedication to living within the Great Sacred Circle.

Stephen Larsen, Ph.D
author of *The Shaman's Doorway, The Mythic Imagination,*
and, with Robin Larsen, *A Fire in the Mind: The Life of Joseph Campbell*

---

[1] The idea of the four peoples of the world, red, yellow, black and white is contained in the Hopi prophesies (See Frank Waters, *The Book of the Hopi*) and is also included in Black Elk's visions.

Acknowledgements

This book was written as an expression of respect, gratitude, responsiblity, and love for those women and men who practice healing within the sacred circle. As I write, I am aware of the voices of many shamanic healers and elders who have touched my spiritual journey: Ikuko Osumi, Takafumi Okagima, Vusamazulu Credo Mutwa, Mama Mona Ndzekeli, Reverend L. F. Ndzekeli, Mashimelo, Mother Sangoma, and numerous other sangomas throughout Southern Africa, Richard, Twele, Chief Mantaga, and the many Bushman healers of the Central Kalahari, Reverend Jerry McAfee, the deacons and church mothers of New Salem Missionary Baptist Church, Panta Leon Rios, Ava Guyrapa Yvoty, Guillermo Rojas, Ava Tape Miri, Ava Veravy Yu, William Tall Bull, Francis Brown, John Hill, Gary and Rita Holy Bull, Ron Geyshick, Dave Gehue, the Mide of northern Minnesota, and my good friend, Sam Gurnoe.

I can not begin to express my thanks to those who contributed in many different ways to my journeys around the world. These include Peter and Ansie Johnson, Stan Lifschitz, Derek and Sanet Shirley, Carol Phillips, Charlie Monkman and Connie Forbister, George Simard, Fernando and Teresa Fernandez-Andes, Viviana Vammalle, Miguel Chase-Sardi, Dora Schnitman, Saul Ignacio Fuks, Sylvia Rechulski, Maggie Carvalho, Senator Armando De Nucci, Burton Foreman, Edward Matsuo, Kenji Kameguchi, Rick Lightning, Dianne Meili, Jeanne Stodola, Chris Loegering, Reverend Virgil Foote, Billy Steele, Camelia and LaShonta Wade, Ron and Deni Simon, M. Vera Bührmann, Christa Zettel, John Sandbach, Richard Katz, Elaine Pagels, the National Anthropological Archives, Smithsonian Institution, and the National Park Service at Pipestone National Monument.

This story never would have been written (and re-written) without the encouragement of Jo Ann Miller, Paul Trachtman, Tullio Maranhão, James Morris, James May, Wendel Ray, Frank Thomas, Margaret Reif, Mary Ann Cincotta, Kate Gurnoe, Steve Parker, Sarah Lagos, Gregg Eichenfield, Skip Nolan, Bill Madsen, Robert Qualls, Ed McGaa, Cynthia Bend, Amy Cordova, Marian Louwagie, Linda Taylor, Trudi Taylor, Gerry Rademeyer, Ricky Snyders, Rich Garland, Jim Nelson, Kathleen O'Sullivan, Rita Gorman, and Diana Whitney. A very special note of appreciation is extended to Tiffany Hand who volunteered to type the original manuscript and was a major source of support for the entire project.

I am particularly grateful to George and Susan Quasha, Chuck Stein, and the staff of Station Hill Press. Their guidance, understanding, caring, and support have been prodigious. This book was meant to be in their hands.

And finally, I want to express gratitude to my family. My grandfather, Reverend W. L. Keeney, was a holy man whose life was an inspiration to all who knew him. I was often aware of his pervasive spiritual presence when I wrote the book. My grandmother, Virginia Keeney, has been a spiritual oasis of great calm, strength, and encouragement. Reverend W. P. Keeney, my father, is largely responsible for instilling my own sense of rallying for people and cultures who struggle against injustice. Phyllis, my mother, is an educator and eternal optimist who taught me that all things are possible to those who practice unbending faith and disciplined work. I also acknowledge how the gifts of her father, Auburn, an eccentric inventor and iconoclast, and her musically talented mother, Bessie, have contributed to my own identity. My sister, Janice, is my tutor regarding how the world can never get enough absurdity and outrageous humor. To my son, Scott, I am thankful for the many ways he teaches me how to live and what to live for. And to my wife, Marian, I am eternally grateful for her healing presence, love, and companionship on our sacred walk together.

Prologue

You came from afar, borne on swept-back Wings of Flame –
A shining Knight seeking the jewelled Grail –
Of timeless Knowledge left by the Ones of Yore;
Long had you travelled, and long endured the pain –
Oh ULYSSES of these electron years –
Ere you arrived at my sylvan abode!
There, near LATLAMORENG's pollution-tainted lake –
Where I have built a dream that will not live –
We briefly shared the Secrets of the Gods.
Grey hours flew by, and soon the Time to Part –
Arrived as does the wrinkled Witch of Death
You took your leave and I was left alone.
When you were gone a Voice spoke in my mind
The voice of One I love and call my Light –
The Mother Goddess, she of a Thousand Names; –
"Doubt not my child 'twas I that brought that man –
From a distant land to the doorstep of your home –
That he may learn from you and you from him –
For Knowledge is a stream that hath no end
You cannot say, in your grey and sunset years –
'KNOWLEDGE IS ENDED, BEHOLD MY TASK IS DONE!'
For you must learn 'till Death closes your eyes
And beyond Death you shall be learning still!
The time has come, my child, the hour is here –
When Truth-Seekers must form a Wall of Shields
Shoulder to shoulder against the coming Foe
Which is Disease, dark Ignorance and War!
You must UNITE! All shamans must join hands
Across the width of this green, tumbling sphere
You know as Earth; my pure life-giving Womb!
No matter how far the skies or wide the seas
You must join hands and start the Dance of Life!

The Drums must sound the plaintive flutes must keen
And the Ritual Fire within the Stone-Circle must blaze
Death must be crushed and foul Illness vanquished
And War be banished from the villages of men!
That is my Command, that is my Word to all!"

Written for Shaking Out the Spirits *by* **Vusamazulu Credo Mutwa**,
High Sanusi and Guardian of Zulu Tribal History and Tribal Relics
Lotlamoreng Dam Traditional Village, Rra-Mosadi-MAFIKENG,
Republic of Bophuthatswana

Sangoma's hut in Mafikeng, Bophuthatswana

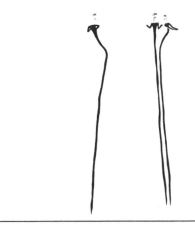

Call of the Sacred Feathers
an Introduction

This story is an account of the experiences leading me from the tamed world of being a university professor to becoming an initiate into ancient healing traditions. Although I never was an anthropologist, researcher, or student of shamanism, years ago I found myself in the midst of experiencing "shamanic realities." Without hallucinogens, spiritual teachers, or esoteric practices, I began having visions leading me to holy women and men in all four corners of the globe. This odyssey began in a quiet Midwestern university town and carried me to medicine people and shamans among North and South American Indians; Christians in the African American Sanctified Baptist Church; sangomas, sanusis, and healers throughout Africa, including the Bushmen of the Kalahari and the Zulu of Southern Africa; and to the only living masters of a pre-Buddhist healing art in Japan. In 1992, when I began telling a few people about my shamanic journeys, some colleagues warned me about going public. They said the story might harm my professional reputation as a scholar. In addition, several medicine people gave warnings about being around other shamans and healers. They spoke of spiritual jealousies and advised seeking protection. These warnings made me reluctant to tell the story.

At the peak of my frustration, a very powerful vision came of a wooden stick in a particular shape with a specified number of feathers on it. I had no idea what this object was but was shaken by the clarity and power of what I had seen. A month later I had several dreams of being told to ask a Guarani Indian shaman about some colored feathers and was shown in the dream how to make the sacred object.

I sent word to my friends and colleagues in Paraguay that I needed to make contact with the Guarani Indians. They contacted Oscar, an anthropologist and ecologist helping the Indians fight to reclaim their land, and he sent my request to the Indians. Cautious about all interactions with white people, the Indian leaders chose someone to "check me out." This resulted in an encounter with three Indian leaders who subsequently arranged a meeting with the President of all the Indian people in Paraguay, Antonio Portillo, a chief whose Indian name is Ava Guyrapa Yvoty.

We met in a shelter outside Asuncion, Paraguay. There I told him I was accepted as a brother of my North American Indian friends. My close friend, Sam, the first Native American medicine man I had gone to for help, advised me to speak as a brother and send the message that the North American Indian people stand with their South American relatives in the struggle to preserve the old ways. I went on to say that some of the holy medicine people of North America wanted to meet them.

Antonio was touched by this greeting and gave a message to me to carry back to the North American Indians, saying their spiritual leaders are now ready to meet with the spiritual leaders of North American Indians. This was the hope of their elders.

I then began telling Antonio about my shamanic journey and the dreams that brought me to him. He replied, "That's what I was waiting to hear." "Come with me." We then went to a room away from everyone else. An elder shaman entered, covered with a full display of shamanic instruments. Things were told about the preservation of their spiritual ways and a prayer was given. I was subsequently invited to sing a prayer. While standing, I held onto the arms of both Antonio and the elder shaman and allowed the spirits to sing a prayer while my hands and body shook from its force. Afterwards, Antonio, with tears in his eyes, said, "This is a very special moment. I must take you to the communities to see how we pray. There you may talk to the shamans and holy fathers. They will tell you about your dreams."

Several days later we took off on an expedition organized by my colleagues, Fernando and Teresa. Antonio was our guide and he first took us to visit a holy man, Guillermo Rojas, in Comunidad Acaraymi, located about 15 kilometers from Iguazu Falls, a territory made familiar by the movie, *The Mission*. This community still practiced the ancient ways and was largely uncontaminated by white religion. There were no missionaries, electricity, or white culture. Here was a community trying to pray and work together in the way they had since the beginning of their culture.

Author with Guillermo Rojas, Guarani "Holy Father"

They had been studied by the anthropologist, Miguel Chase-Sardi, whose book, *El Precio De La Sangre*, had a photograph of the elder shaman, Guillermo Rojas, on its cover.

A week before, I had met with Miguel asking whether he had ever seen the object I dreamed. He said he never had, but if anyone knew, it would be a certain distinguished anthropologist who had written many books on the Guarani Indians. He called her and described the object. She emphatically replied, "I have never seen such a thing. It does not exist!"

I looked at Vivian, my translator, and Fernando and thought of the first day of my arrival in Paraguay. On that day I had met Oscar, the man who initially made contact with the Indians for us. When he heard a bit of the dream he said we needed to go to a special shop where crafts made by the Guarani Indians are sold. When we arrived I noticed that behind the owner's desk was the object I had dreamed. Although the feathers were of a different color, the shape of the stick and the number of feathers were the same. At that instant I knew my dreams had led me to the right place. The shop clerk said the object was recently brought to them by a shaman with the instructions not to sell it. On the first day in Paraguay, Vivian, Fernando, Oscar, and I all had seen the shamanic object several anthropologists claimed did not exist. A great mystery was set in motion.

The following week took us to the village of Comunidad Acaraymi where a gathering of their spiritual leaders took place. A large thatch roofed structure with open sides housed an altar in front of a long wooden canoe. On the altar were many sacred feathers and shamanic items. Prayers and dancing were conducted and the shaman baptised us with holy water from a spiritual canoe.

Antonio asked me to sing my prayer. I touched the shaman and allowed the spirits to sing through me. Afterwards, Guillermo Rojas, the shaman, blew on me and moved his feathers over my body. He said, "You have really prayed. I have seen your heart. You are a holy man." When I told him my visions, he replied, "This vision only comes to a holy person. You are a messenger who must say things to the world. You are to tell people that the old spiritual ways have to survive. It is now time for the spiritual leaders from different parts of the world to meet and pray together for the survival of the earth. You are at home and safe with the Indian peoples of the world. They recognize you as a holy man. You need to be careful around white people. I will give you protection and put you under the watch of our community." He then gave me his bracelet covered with many feathers for protection.

I was both disturbed and comforted by the elder shaman's words. I felt uncomfortable being described as a "holy man" and did not receive his words as a characterization of me, but as a serious and disturbing challenge to live a more sacred life. At the same time, I was comforted by the holy man's gifts of protection. I was able to continue the journey in Paraguay with revitalized strength and commitment. After another day of traveling in the semi-tropical forests of Paraguay, we came to Antonio's village, Curuguaty, in Comunidad Fortuna. There we met his father, Floricio Portillo, and his uncle, Florencio Portillo. Both were shamans and led the community in preserving the ancient traditions.

In the first days of trying to make contact with the Indians prior to meeting Antonio, Oscar reported an unusual occurrence. A young boy without any money traveled from the forest and somehow managed to arrive at his office. The boy said, "My father believes you have a message for him." Oscar had no idea how the boy was able to find him but discovered the boy's father was a very great shaman, a man called the "priest of the forest." Oscar began wondering whether this was the shaman I should meet. A week later, upon our arrival at Antonio's village, the same young

Author with Ava Tape Miri, Guarani "Priest of the Forest"

boy was present. His father was Antonio's uncle, the "priest of the forest." His Indian name was Ava Tape Miri, meaning "small seagull man." When I first saw his face I recognized the man I had seen in my vision.

Soon after our arrival, the community gathered for a ceremony at the sacred temple and altar, which was in front of Florencio's house. When Florencio prayed, his voice conveyed a sincerity opening everyone's heart. His presence was remarkably holy and healing. He told the community he had dreamed of my coming and of what I would say. Both Florencio and Floricio told the community that it was God that spoke through me when I prayed my holy song. They, too, believed my mission was to help bring the different ancient traditions together. They had seen how the world is dying and that only a return to practicing the old spiritual ways could save it. Some of these Indian people were already building their canoes in preparation for the next great cleansing. There was very little time left for the old ways to be saved. I was told the spirits of the Guarani Indians would protect and strenghten me if I followed my spiritual call. If I did not, there would be no protection. Florencio gave me his necklace for protection and proceeded to conduct three hours of ceremonial praying and dancing. Antonio held a portable tape recorder to tape my conversation with Florencio. I told the story of my shamanic journey, the visions leading me to South America, and sang a holy song. Because there is no electricity or phones in most of the Indian villages throughout Paraguay, communication takes place via radio broadcasts. On Saturday mornings Indian communities gather around radios to hear news relevant to them. Antonio was taping this encounter to be broadcast to all the Indians in Paraguay.

Following the evening ceremonies, Florencio said he would tell me at sunrise about my visions. That evening I dreamed of Florencio, seeing his face with eyes that reflected a great fire. The sound of a man grunting awakened me. I looked and saw Florencio at a distance staring into a fire he had just built. When I told him my dream, he replied that he has the ability to "dream me" and that he is always available to me in that world.

The next morning Florencio said that what I saw in my earlier visions was something very holy to his people. All holy people in his culture dream of a particular stick with feathers. They must then make it and hold it in their hand. It is used for healing and can not be touched by anyone other than the one who dreamed it. Kept in one's home, it offers strong protection for one's family. I asked if he would help me find the stick and feathers. Immediately he went into the forest and returned with the exact stick I had dreamed. He then went to the roof above the altar and pulled out the feathers I needed. He said, "Now you must make it and hold it in your hand. Then you will have another vision."

Florencio and I became connected as spiritual brothers. I feel I have always known him. It is beyond my ability to understand how our dreams brought us together. Becoming accepted as a brother to the Guarani Indians solidified my commitment to following the spiritual path. Whatever the consequences may be for my "professional reputation," I must walk the path of doing all I can to protect, preserve, and practice the old ways. I am connected to the ancestors of Antonio and Florencio and not a day goes by without my acknowledging these relationships. They give me strength and protection to carry on the journey. I now know that saving the old ways and saving the earth are the same. It is time to reconnect with the sacred circle of healing and pray for all the spiritual traditions circumscribing Mother Earth.

I have described my journeys in a truthful manner and have revealed what was given to share and have not spoken about matters not to be known. The spirits have called for the release of these words and understandings. Elder practitioners of ancient healing traditions throughout the world have given me messages to share with others. In this regard, I am only a messenger passing on wisdom articulated and blessed by practitioners of the old ways.

Author with Ava Guyrapa Yvoty, President of the Guarani Indians

The Beginning Vision

The story most seriously began in 1971 when I was nineteen years old. At that time, an unusual experience challenged my whole life. What I am about to describe took place during the month of January when a noteworthy weather change happened in a small Midwestern town named Columbia, Missouri. Following months of perilously cold temperatures, ice storms, and blizzards, the sun broke through the clouds and created a week of perfect summer weather, what the locals called the most incredible Indian summer within anyone's memory.

One early evening during this particular week, I walked the streets within and around the university, fully enjoying the gift of summer in the midst of winter. Unknown to me at the time, I walked in front of a building holding the original notes and manuscripts of the interviews conducted by John Neihardt with Black Elk, the holy Oglala Sioux medicine man. Inside that building were shorthand notes recorded in four spiral notebooks that constituted the first written record of what has become known as one of the greatest spiritual visions in history. When I stood in front of that building, I never had heard of Black Elk. Furthermore, I knew nothing about visions, mysticism, or anything that went "bump in the night." For reasons I'm still trying to understand, something happened that evening, changing my life forever, starting me on a journey that continues through this day. After passing by the place holding the manuscript of Black Elk's sacred vision, I was taken over by an all pervasive sense of peace, calm, and silent knowing. This possession of calmness led me to the nearest building that was open, the university chapel. It had been years since I had been in a church and I never had been inside the chapel I now entered.

I moved without any sense of conscious direction and found myself sitting in the front row of the chapel. There I began to experience a sensation of heat at the base of my spine. It did not startle or frighten me since

I felt the previous hours of peace, calm, and knowing had been preparation for what was about to occur. My whole being became concentrated upon this experience. The inner heat smoothly climbed up my back and I looked up and turned toward the left corner of the chapel. The heat inside me came through my head and was transformed into a white light. It moved into the corner of the chapel where I fixed my gaze and became a circular-like screen of white light within which I had a vision. I was absolutely unaware of anything else in the chapel. After the experience, I assumed no one else had been there except my girlfriend who later said others had come to the chapel and had become concerned and frightened by my "out of touch with the world" appearance. No one could communicate with me, and I had no awareness of anyone. All my focus, sensory experience, and being were directed upon the vision within the white light. In this vision I saw and experienced one image after another of suffering and healing. I saw the face of Jesus, Gandhi, and others whose lives had been devoted to helping heal those who suffer. My body and hands shook and I wept deeply throughout the experience. I felt called to participate in this tradition of service. In a riveting way the vision showed that other realities or ways of being existed. Without question the experience initiated a transformation of my life.

One of the most unusual aspects of what happened is that I am unable to remember, even to this day, some of what I was shown during that evening. I do know that what I beheld was so sacred and powerful that it caused me to weep and shake for most of the night.

I sat in this state for several hours and then left the chapel. I wandered around for a while and ended up in another church. When I sat down and looked up, the vision continued. The white light was always present. I feared the over-powering strength of it and tried to keep looking down. My hands were very hot —they seemed as hot as coals — and I felt I could heal with them.

I also had the sense that I could answer any question that I was asked. There was no self-indulgence in this awareness. I simply regarded it as a natural consequence of the state I was in. The experience was so large, so sacred, and so holy, that I was absolutely unaware of my own identity. What was all important and all present was the vision. I wept, prayed, and struggled to control the vision throughout the entire night.

I had enough wisdom to keep quiet about what was going on. I stayed away from priests, ministers, rabbis, therapists, counselors, and all other professional people helpers. There was little doubt they would not understand. My response to the continuing presence of the vision was to remain still and to allow the vision to digest and calm down. About a month later, I could safely look up again without the heavens being opened.

As soon as I was able, I rushed to the bookstores and tried to find something to explain what had happened. One of the first books I found was the autobiographical account of the yogi, Gopi Krishna, who had what he called a "spontaneous kundalini awakening." When I read his description of experiencing heat moving up his spine, I knew something natural had happened to me. Unfortunately, his heat turned into a fire that hurt him. The inner fire, or what he called "kundalini energy," was nothing to play around with. Inappropriate activation and utilization of it, he argued, could lead to bodily harm. I vowed to stop reading anything else about this experience, largely because reading about it helped activate it. I decided to move on with my life.

I kept the story of this visionary experience to myself for thirteen years. In 1984 I finally told it to Stafford Beer, an internationally renowned cybernetician, poet, and yoga teacher. He immediately replied, "You have been blessed and given what many spiritual disciples devote a lifetime to receiving."

In those thirteen years of silence, I managed to move from coast to coast with many stops in between. While my journey during this silence carried me to many places, I always knew I was being led and prepared for something. The memory of that great vision pervaded all I did, even though I had no idea what really had happened.

Preparation and Incubation

I became a university professor whose academic work was connected to "systemic" and "ecological" thinking. These ideas lead one to a broader understanding of mind. Here mind is not limited to being contained within the boundaries of a brain but may be understood as circumscribed by a conversation, dance, forest, or a whole biosphere. The pattern connecting you and me may become a mind transcending the limitations of our individually marked cerebral cortices. Making such "I-Thou" connections is the process of creating mind(s). My years of learning to see mind in relationships and in nature helped prepare me for returning to my beginning vision and the shamanic mind of healing.

In studying what Gregory Bateson called the "ecology of mind," I became more aware of how people, performing artists in particular, were searching for ways of moving beyond the limitations of their every-day, predictable minds. They sought experience that was "spontaneous," "creative," "original," and "improvisational." Such experience came when their every-day mind was connected to another, whether the other be another person, musical instrument, or paint brush, so as to create a mind larger than what they knew as their "own." In the surrender of their own mind to this larger mind, they would behold the gifts and surprises of creative, improvisational conduct.

As my academic career developed over the years, I moved from being principally concerned with understanding the mind of improvisation and creativity to becoming an improvisational performer myself, particularly in the context of therapy and teaching. Accordingly, improvisation became both the topic and process of my approach. In working with therapists, I sometimes invited them to give me one sentence a client might utter like, "I'm so depressed I can't go to work." I would then improvise an entire therapy session giving expression to both the voices of client and therapist. What was surprising in these improvised therapy plays was that occasionally someone in the class would say, "You just described the very situation of my own life." Being open, which is what improvisation requires, can lead to picking up information from sources one doesn't know about. My wildest offering to therapeutic improvisation took place in Florida. While there, the governor of the state was embarrassed by an exposé on the state mental hospital, which made the front page of the *Miami Herald*. It showed how the place was rather barbaric and wasn't even accredited. In response, the governor formed a committee to do something about it.

I got into this situation as a consultant. It didn't take long to learn that many mental health consultants at the highest levels are basically lobbyists for building construction companies. Almost every recommendation to the head of the state hospital involved constructing or remodeling a building.

When I had an opportunity to speak, I asked what kind of trees were on the hospital grounds. The administrator responded, "litchi trees." "Aren't litchi nuts very expensive and rare?" I asked. "Yes, indeed." "They are a delicacy" was the response.

I suggested the state hospital construct a bakery to sell litchi nuts and other nuts grown on the state hospital grounds. It was especially important, I added, that the bakery specialize in making fruit cakes with these nuts. "Fantastic!" the chief hospital administrator exclaimed to my great surprise. "The governor's wife has been trying to get us to implement 'agritherapy.'" However, the idea of outsiders driving into the state hospital to purchase fruit cakes and nuts grown on a nut farm was too much for the other committee members. It was my last invitation to attend the meetings!

I did manage to improvise one other proposal, however. In Florida there was a long list of so-called "mentally ill" people waiting, sometimes for years, to enter the overcrowded facility. I suggested interviewing the people on that waiting list and finding those who had managed to stay out of trouble and keep their lives in reasonably decent shape. These people could be hired to teach other people on the waiting list how to survive prior to getting in. Some might even learn enough survival tactics to avoid having to enter the hospital altogether. That was my last consultation with the symbiotic world of building contractors and state hospitals.

I had learned how to improvise as a teacher, therapist, consultant, and writer but now wanted to make it happen with music on a keyboard. Music, particularly jazz piano, was one of my greatest passions. Unfortunately, I practically had stopped playing the piano when I was in my early twenties. This was partly due to my belief that it helped "stir up" mystical experience. When I was nineteen, I had begun composing music and this seemed to be connected to opening me to the powerful vision that took place then. When I now, sixteen years later, decided to learn musical improvisation, I began wondering whether any shamanic doors would again open.

Rather than finding a teacher and going through the laborious path of practicing scales and memorizing chords, I decided to try an experiment. I tried to learn jazz by the following formula. First, I kept the "fire of desire" alive by always remembering to turn to a record or concert when I was feeling discouraged or less motivated. Second, I sat in front of the keyboard and waited for something to happen. And finally, I encouraged my belief that something could in fact happen that would lead me to the territory of jazz. Paradoxically, sometimes what would happen was the learning of a scale or chord configuration.

While learning jazz improvisation, I met a woman who had been studied and written about as a pure case of synesthesia, that is, her sensory experiences were typically not limited to one form of sensation at a time. For instance, she saw light shows when she heard music, often seeing shapes on a screen about six inches in front of her face.

This woman's passion was jazz and as we became more acquainted it was remarkable that my way of learning to play jazz was similar to her experience of sensing it. I was entering a state of mind enabling me to approach playing as a kind of internalized geography where chords could be "grabbed" more than calculated or heard. Playing was a kinesthetic-visual-auditory feat not entirely organized by conscious knowledge of music. Our conversations about listening to jazz resulted in bringing us closer to one another. One day we sat down and stared at one another's eyes with an immovable, intense focus. We each viewed the other as changing right before us. I saw her as old, as young, as another person, and as various other creatures. These were not dream images but were experienced as actual shifts of perception taking place in front of us. In this interpersonal space, energy in the form of shaking and heat returned to my body.

After many years, the shamanic door opened again. For several months in 1988 we would meet with each other almost daily to do whatever it was we were doing. Our practice usually had the same form. We would hold each other in our arms, stare into the other's eyes, and I would begin shaking. The shaking was like different forms of vibration. It often began in my solar plexus and then spread throughout the whole of my body. There was a sense of being filled with energy and having my body used for this dance of vibrating patterns. On several occasions the choreography of shaking and vibrating culminated in a cosmic-like experience where my entire head felt like it was shot into space. Years later I found this experience was not unknown to particular forms of Buddhist practice. The practice of vibrating reopened my relation to nonordinary worlds. In the evening I often found when I retired that the whole bed began shaking. Sometimes I was awakened in the middle of the night by tremors so violent that it felt like it was caused by a major earthquake. There were times when this activity seriously frightened me. One evening I faced what appeared as an evil spirit and felt it was possible to die that very moment. After crying out for spiritual help, it eventually became safe again.

I began to see trees and plants vibrate, to see them move, as if they, too, were breathing or dancing in these rhythms. The music, meanwhile, was developing and becoming what was clearly jazz improvisation. Without knowing how I did it, I was playing jazz. I didn't know all the chords, didn't play by ear, but could feel myself around a geography of grabbing keys and riding the pulse of a song. A tape of this music was produced and a public radio station aired a selection. As my practice of this way of being continued, it became clear that there was no particular context for grounding it. I was living twenty-four hours a day in a world filled with nonordinary experiences. The culturally ordinary world had become foreign and I began to worry about where all this would lead. In learning to improvise with my words, music, and body, I became more open to uncommon experience. Having prepared and incubated in these ways, I was ready for a new way of being.

Sweat and Purification

In 1989 an opportunity to occupy a professorship where I could limit myself to teaching and writing soon presented itself. The job came from the northern United States, where I had seven years earlier met an Ojibway medicine man who felt like a "soul brother." The job opportunity seemed like no accident and I accepted. Within months of moving, I met with this man and told him my story. I said I could no longer run away from whatever had been chasing me. I now vibrated, had visions, and unconsciously improvised music on a regular basis. In the traditional way of offering tobacco, I asked for his help. In ceremony he explained where he came from, how he was part of a medicine lodge, and gave me instructions as to what would take place. He "smudged" us, brought forth his sacred objects, drummed, and sang his songs. In a dream he saw me isolated on a bluff covered with a blanket and shivering in the rain. He explained I was being called to go on a vision fast. He described the blanket I was to go find and said he knew where the place in the dream was located.

Over the next seven months, I prayed for guidance and help. I was prepared for the vision fast through participation in a sweat lodge. In my first sweat, the medicine man noted the sound of an eagle inside the lodge. The fire tender later reported an eagle had flown over us during that time.

The rocks in this sweat lodge generated more heat than I ever imagined a human body enduring. Fear for one's immediate survival and ability to withstand the heat quickly burned out any trivial concerns and considerations. All of us were leveled to the ground as creatures with an equal desire to live. The sacred door of a sweat is opened when one surrenders one's will to the heat of the stones. One gives up fighting the heat and allows it to be one with oneself. There is simply no other way to survive an exceptionally hot sweat. It helps to acknowledge and respect the fact that the stones actually give up their lives to help one live. When this transformation of one's relationship to the heat takes place, the simple structure of a dome made up of willow branches and blankets is transformed into the most sacred cathedral on earth. The presence of the holy is brought forth in a way no architect of a flying buttress ever imagined possible.

In this sweat, several of us began singing in an unfamiliar language. All of us prayed with full hearts. A light filled the top of the dome and the experience of spirit was felt by everyone. In my desire to be good, I asked the spirits for forgiveness of the sins and crimes white people had committed against Native American people. I asked that I help pay for the sins of my people. The next day my body began developing what looked like serious burns. The doctor couldn't understand what had happened to me, saying it looked like the worst case of poison oak he had ever seen. I suffered for several months with raw, oozing open flesh all over my body. When I was finally healed, the medicine man reminded me that next time I do not have to ask to take on the sins of my people. I could simply ask the spirits to take pity. I learned the importance of choosing my words carefully when addressing the spirits.

The lessons learned in a sweat lodge can be learned in the sweats of living. Sometimes the heat of personal and social crises bears down and one thinks one cannot survive. In the same way one can stop fighting or resisting the heat of the stones, one can stop resisting the pressures, stress, heat, and weight of catastrophic life events whether they involve physical pain, grief, economic ruin, relationship calamities, professional humiliations, or war.

In my career as a psychotherapist, I have been very outspoken against the field of psychiatry. I have argued that the practice of labeling others with psychiatric terms that stigmatize and disempower is wrong. I have held, furthermore, that the frequent dispensing of psychiatric drugs accompanied by the lie that so-called research justifies their use is irresponsible and that locking people up in institutions is not therapy, but police action and social control. I have no doubt that most of what psychiatry addresses are spiritual crises and natural problems in living. The medicalizing and scientizing of these events in people's lives too often strips away opportunities for spiritual work. In the beginning of my career, I was confused, hurt, and often angry with the mental health professions. It often felt as if I were at war with these people and their institutions. It took many, many lessons for me to finally learn that the pain of this sort of conflict is no different than the heat from the stones in a sweat lodge.

My encounter with the possible life-threatening situation of a bone tumor made me sweat even more and learn the value of having the presence of death as a resource for living. Staring at the inevitability of the end of one's life provides a way of being awakened, fully awakened, to the present realization of being alive. Some people diagnosed as "terminally ill" are often more alive in their final months than people who live a full life span without ever experiencing and knowing their aliveness. A minute of being fully alive is more valuable than ninety years as a zombie.

My personal relationships have also provided many difficult lessons about how one cannot control much of anything. I lived many years in a relationship where life at home consisted mainly of the search for my partner's hidden bottles of alcohol and protecting myself from unpredictable outbursts. There I was, an internationally recognized expert on helping other families in crisis, helpless and defeated in my own home. Although I was successful in keeping the arms of psychiatry and the police out of the household, I was unable to stop the action of a team of lawyers who dragged me through the divorce courts with all the cruelty and economic persecution our legal system permits. My life, as I had known it, was taken away.

I fully empathize with those who have been in impossible relationship crises, whether in their marriage, family, neighborhood, or work place. Perhaps the greatest temptation is to hate and attack those who have unjustly done harm to one and one's family. How difficult it is to resist the path of fighting and turn to the spiritual way of trying to imagine walking in your opponent's moccasins. To take the next step, loving one's enemy, requires a miracle, perhaps the greatest miracle of any spiritual journey. I was once threatened by the chairman of my university department, who warned he would destroy me because I asked too many questions. Subsequently my office was repeatedly broken into, initiating a campaign of intimidation and terrorism. The evil perpetuated through back-stabbing gossip, lying, deception, outright crime, and even death threats has not left me unscathed.

The world is full of such cruelty and ugliness and it is not limited to the large-scale profit-making institutions. Corruption is also rampant in small non-profit social agencies and religious organizations whose mission is to serve those who have great need. I am deeply saddened and angered when I consider how many gifted and creative students, teachers, and aspiring professionals I have observed being destroyed by the use of gossip and coalitionary politics. Typically the only reasons for this destruction are personal jealousy and the raw desire to exercise power over others. Sometimes it's easier to dodge fists and bullets than it is to reckon with the poisonous nature of inappropriate social coalitions and villifying, duplicitous gossip. Today's "social plague" may be the rampant spread of the gossip virus into our social institutions. It is time to recognize the dangers gossip poses, whether speaking or listening to it, and to acknowledge the extent to which it has invaded and is destroying our society.

In the story that follows, I have chosen not to dwell on the details of my own suffering and hardships. This has been done ably before in the spiritual stories of other lives. It is enough to say I also have experienced many of the depths of hell through being attacked by stupid cruelty, pathological jealousy, and painful insanity. In suffering I found no choice but to surrender to a spiritual journey. Having lost almost everything I thought important, I felt I had little to lose. Having been brought down by the fires of pain, I plunged as deeply as I could into the healing waters of the oldest spiritual wells. I did not approach any spiritual tradition out of curiosity. I went because life had broken me down and I knew no other place to turn.

In my physical, occupational, economic, and relational crises, I learned that the most basic spiritual lessons articulated by the great spiritual traditions cannot be recited enough. The sweats of our lives teach us these simple old truths when we are open to hearing them:

1. We simply are not intelligent or wise enough to judge any one.
2. The most powerful and transforming medicine is to forgive and love our enemies.
3. Recognize and accept one's unimportance. Fools Crow, the great Teton Sioux medicine man, considered himself "lower than any condemned man anywhere" and never exalted himself above anyone. Each of us has committed every sin, if not in our conduct, then in our thoughts.
4. Acknowledge the equality of all living things. Plants are as sacred as human beings.
5. Shifting focus from self to relationship brings forth the understanding that giving is the most satisfying gift.
6. The highest call is to be used, not to use.

7. All spiritual blessings you receive and create are to be released and given to others. This way of passing it on makes us transformers of spirit. In this way we are transformed.

Vision Fast

About a month before the vision fast for which the sweat was a preparation, I was awakened between 4:00 and 5:00 a.m., the time when many spiritual events take place for me. I looked up and to the left of my bed was standing an old Indian medicine man. I must have seen his face before in a book because he looked familiar. He was in full ceremonial attire, had long hair, and was absolutely still. Only later would I find out who he was.

I was startled at the ghostlike realism of this perception — the clearest vision I had ever experienced. I was aware of being awake and knew I saw this spirit. Without speaking, he talked to my mind and told me about the pipe. I closed my eyes and was taken to a room with people and was given further instruction.

As the winter of 1989 began to approach its end, the necessary preparations and instruction for the vision fast were given. The best definition of a vision fast is that it is a time marked for praying, crying, and begging for a vision. Native Americans have different ways of conducting this sacred ritual. All involve the location of a sacred site away from civilization enabling the vision faster to be in direct contact with nature. Some traditions specify digging a hole in the ground, while others prescribe a special way of marking a spot. I was taken to a sacred area by the medicine man. Following a day's journey, we located the area and got out to explore. My task was to ask for guidance to the specific spot. As we were walking, an eagle flew over us and landed in an area I understood as my spot. The medicine man sang holy songs, prayed, and made offerings at the site. The next day involved final preparations for the fast. A sweat lodge was built for my return from the fast. I received the acknowledgements and prayers of several local Indian people and was given instructions as to how my spot was to be prepared with colored flags and offerings. At sunrise my face was marked with black stripes, my shoes filled with cedar, and I was given the pipe I had been told to hold in the previous sweat. Prayers were made and I was taken to the end of the road to make the final hike. With brotherly love, the medicine man told me he was proud of me for doing what I was doing and gave me an eagle feather he had fasted with, which had been given to him by an elder. He told me to never let go of that feather and pipe. His final words were, "Be brave." After a silent hug, I walked on.

When I came close to the bluff where I was to sit, a deer that had been resting there came charging out. A bolt of energy filled me with nervous anticipation of what was to come. Following the necessary preparations and offerings, I began my prayers for vision. The day was beautiful and sunny and within minutes more birds than I had ever seen in my life sang and sang. I couldn't pray, the music was too much to ignore. I sat in this concert listening to their songs while some flew immediately over me from tree to tree. Their performance put me to sleep that afternoon. When I awoke, I looked out and my first awareness was of an eagle flying by. I watched its majestic flight and felt it belonged to a world different from that of the other creatures. I went back to my prayers and fell asleep again. Upon awakening, the eagle was there. This pattern recurred throughout the whole time. Every time I awakened from dozing off, the eagle was there. Some of the time there were two eagles flying together.

As the sun began to leave the day, it was as if a lifetime had passed. Nature's preparation for evening was a ritual unsurpassed in its cadence and delivery. New songs and sounds prepared a different time and place, that of the night. As dark settled in, the sound of creatures crawling around became unnerving. I prayed for courage to accept whatever would be presented. I was not prepared for how cold it can become sitting outside on a cliff at night. No amount of clothes could keep that cold wind from getting to my bones. I covered myself with my blanket and fell asleep briefly, only to be awakened by the song of a coyote that was about eight feet away from me. I then knew who had taught the Indian to sing. It is a singing for spiritual practice. I dared not move—being that close to a coyote was not in my repetoire of conduct. I simply sat and absorbed the song. When the coyote finished, I noticed, *really* noticed, the sky. Never before had I seen a sky so unlittered by the light pollution of civilization. The stars were alive in their clarity.

I was grateful for being alive and for the gifts of song and beauty that had come forth. I reflected on a thought that had come to me that afternoon. As complicated as we think our lives are, when isolated in nature it doesn't take long to bankrupt every idea, thought, worry, reflection on the past, present, and future our mind is capable of creating. The bigger silence of the outside quickly stills the noise of our inside.

Having never really camped outside in my life, I was not aware of how quickly conditions can change. Out of nowhere clouds came and covered the moon and stars. Frightening sounds came near me, including a stomping on the ground that made the earth shake. I was quickly catapulted into wrestling with raw, naked, unadulterated fear. The status of a human being, I quickly learned, could easily be leveled to that of a blade of grass when the pretend protective structures of civilization are vacated. It became very, very cold and I trembled and prayed throughout the rest of the night. I begged for the sun to come out. I now understood why the sun had been worshipped throughout the ages.

When that first light of morning crept into the skyline, I danced a celebration for its bringing a new day with the possibility of warmth and light. Thanksgiving was in order, and I soon fell asleep with eager anticipation of another day. When I awakened, the world had changed. The sun was gone and a fog was everywhere. There was so much fog I couldn't tell whether I was still asleep in a dream or not. And then the eagle came. Coming closer than it ever had before, it flew as a distinct presence in the fog. I honored it with all the feeling in my heart. My heart's fill of feeling could not be contained, and a song came out of me unlike any sound or song I had ever made. Prior to that moment, I was not a singer and did not sing. But I sang then with all the sound that a human being can make. My heart sang to this eagle and in this singing I was connected with its flight. I felt the beingness of that eagle and felt flight. The eagle taught me something no book ever could. We may become one with each other through the wings of our hearts. This singing and seeing is from the "I" of the heart, not from the rationed rationales of rational mind. I sang, danced, flew, and became indistinguishable from the eagle, finally going to its spot in the tree. I was full. I did not want anything else. I had received more than I possibly could have imagined.

The fog and the wind then began to churn with a force that threatened my staying in one place. The wind was now turning into a storm and I began to worry whether I could survive its impact. I felt I had been given what I was there to receive but also thought a sacrifice was necessary as an expression of my appreciation. The decision was to endure the elements. If cold, powerful wind wasn't enough, it began to rain, first a little and then a lot. There I was, the picture the medicine man had seen in his dream — a shivering wet man under a blanket on a cliff in a storm. I remembered the hot rocks of a sweat lodge and tried to stop fighting the cold. Upon surrendering my resistance, I stripped naked and stood in the elements while dancing and singing. It was a good time to die. A voice inside told me to leave immediately. It was getting near dark and my pride wanted to stay at least another night. The internal voice said, "Leave or you will die." I gave my final offering and walked several miles to a campsite the medicine man had set up. The storm worsened, a lot of the tent's inside was wet and I began fighting hypothermia. I dried myself, changed clothes, and knew I would survive. The next morning I awoke to see the smile of the medicine man. We went to a sweat, I shared my story, and a feast was served. He said, "You are being shown some things."

Becoming an Empty Tube

One of the results of the vision fast during the months that followed was that I began to experience music coming more directly through me. I could imagine a white eagle and experience it playing music through my body. I once visualized a geometrical drawing that began to move and become transformed into a thunderbird. It made me wonder whether those ancient petroglyphs and stone drawings were sacred designs intended to be opened by one's mind into other transformations. The music was unlike anything I had ever played or heard before. Once I felt my face stretching into a different face and my fingers extending as if they were getting longer. I saw myself as an older musician from another era — and the music poured forth in a classical style! I sent a tape to several musicologists who proclaimed that it was in the traditions of Stravinsky, Debussy, and Scriabin.

Ken Werner, one of the premier jazz pianists of our time, gave a lecture at the 1991 International Association of Jazz Educators entitled, "Channeling the Music." He stated that "the music is there already before you play it" and "all you have to do is tap into it and it's going to flow out at such an alarming rate that the task will be to stop it, to shut it off, so you can go to sleep after the gig." He went on to say that "the physical contortions one goes through to play a good solo can lead to actual physical illness if one is trying to make music, rather than let music happen." These insights apply to spiritual practice in general. Spiritual experiences occur naturally and effortlessly when one is open as a channel, or, as Fools Crow put it, as a "hollow bone" or "tube." It comes through you without strenuous exercising or working to make it happen.

This philosophy of playing music applies not only to prayer, chanting, singing, and healing, but all activities of the human imagination. It is the most radical educational idea alive in the world today. If it were taken more seriously, most educational programs and institutions would have to be scrapped and new ones built from scratch. When one becomes a hollow tube and allows spiritual experience to move through, the idea of wrong notes and right notes, or more generally good and evil, is dissipated. As any devoted listener of music can tell you, listening to someone play all the right notes without heart and soul is music that is wrong. On the other hand, playing the wrong note with heart and soul sounds right. When a musician "is played," there are no mistakes, everything is right and the audience always includes the performer.

"Evil," in part, is a name given to the fear of being open. As the boundaries of familiarity are transgressed, we face the unknown. Since we don't know it, we cannot control it. If we cannot relinquish the desire to control, to totally understand, or to concretize our knowing, then facing the unfamiliar may be uncomfortably shocking or even result in a panic. This panic before the unknown can be handled by creating an image of our fear, perhaps a monster or evil spirit, that we then name or christen as "evil." With an ideology that evil is to be avoided and done away with, we justify backing up and avoiding any further confrontation with the unknown, whether in ourselves or with others.

In spiritual work one needs to focus on becoming a clean, empty tube for the spirits to come through. Prayer, sweat, sacrifice, and being nonattached to any material (or nonmaterial) things helps keep one's tube empty and clean.

But preparation of the tube is only half the story. The rest involves getting self out of the way and letting one's empty clean tube be used. When this process is realized and practiced, the healer does not have to fear doing the right or wrong thing. The healer doesn't have to worry about self-importance or embarrassment. In this healing there is no healer, just a clean, empty tube. In this music, there is no musician, just an instrument. Any gloating or self-indulgent reflection after a performance, however, may put a speck of dirt on the wall of the tube. This, in turn, will have to be burned out by the heat of sacred rocks or the fire of prayer. Returning to nothing, time and time again, is always the preparation for the reception of everything.

In the fall of 1990, about a year following my experiments with music, I met a woman, Marian, who had a history of walking a spiritual path. She had a previous encounter with cancer and had learned spiritual lessons from her Christian faith. She was a practicing therapist with a special interest in conducting grief groups. Later I felt a strong urge to invite her to sit with me so that we might open ourselves to the possibility of experiencing a moment of healing. As soon as we sat down, I began to shake and my hand vibrated as it touched her shoulder and head. After meeting Marian, I began exploring the use of body vibrating as a healing practice with others. Sometimes I had the experience of seeing a kind of x-ray image where white lines marked where my hands should go. If people came to me tired or feeling sick, the vibratory work left them with a sense of energy transmission and health. It had both preventative and curative consequences. This kind of confirmation helped move the work forward. It seemed that a new form of bodywork had emerged. It was vibrational, utilized the therapists hands and sometimes the whole body, and was improvisational, that is, different for each situation. The vibrations ranged from a small pulse to huge, convulsion-like shakes. The sessions ranged from minutes to hours.

I found that doing this work with another person could be a way of passing it on. Sometimes the other person would begin vibrating, often beginning with their hands and then moving into other parts of their body. As this practice evolved, I began going into spontaneous vibrational patterns with chanting, singing, and speaking a variety of sounds. I then began using my voice with the body work, sometimes projecting sounds into a person. Day by day this way of healing continued to unfold.

The Search for Context

As the weeks and months passed, I became more and more aware that I was facing a shamanic calling. By March, 1991, the dilemma that presented itself seemed to be, how am I to contextualize this? Is it to be presented as a new body therapy? Does it belong in private practice? Should it be contained as a spiritual healing practice? If so, then in what spiritual tradition? Did it fit any tradition? Should a context be invented for its practice? Marian and I searched for help and soon found ourselves attending an inner-city African American church called, New Salem Missionary Baptist Church. I had heard the minister, the Reverend Jerry McAfee, speak at a community function and had the hunch we should try out his church. We had no idea we would ever join it. We were simply going on the idea this might be an interesting place to visit.

Although I had grown up in a country church, I hadn't been back to a church since the powerful vision I had several decades before. My last contact with Christianity had been when I was an undergraduate in a religious college, editing and publishing an underground newsletter entitled, "For Christ's Sake." It was a radical call for Christian social activism inspired by the theological work of Harvey Cox, Dietrich Bonhoeffer, and Rosemary Ruether. The newsletter resulted in a mob of fundamentalist, right-wing students asking the dean of the college to request that I leave. I gave up on the church at that time and went to the Massachusetts Institute of Technology where I received a scholarship based on my having won a first place award at the International Science Fair when I was a senior in high school. For years I tried to dedicate my life to science and other intellectual pursuits. My academic career became very successful, and my first book, *Aesthetics of Change*, was cited in *The Encyclopedia of Artificial Intelligence* as being one of the major works written on cybernetics.

When we first visited the church at New Salem, it felt like home even though most of the time we were the only white people there. The services invited people to open up to spiritual experience and it was not uncommon for people to spontaneously shout, chant, sing, dance, and sometimes pass out. We joined the church and were baptized in the basement baptismal pool while the church members sang, "Wade in the Water." I remember passing out and turning stiff as a board when I went under water. The pastor, deacon, and I all felt what the deacon called a "lightening bolt" go through me when I was raised.

Several of the members of the church qualify as saints to us. One in particular, Brother Amos Griffin, is a tower of light and a beacon of spiritual love. We asked him to spiritually adopt us. The pastor is unique in how he leads the church to be both the voice of social responsibility for the community while providing a context that nurtures spiritual experience. A church is typically either one or the other, but here social activism and responsibility go hand and hand with "getting dirty for the Lord," as one of the church mothers put it.

The church services would get my spiritual energy cooking. During the service, my body would shake, often coming from the base of my spine. The shaking was sometimes so natural I thought someone else was rocking the pew. At times I have almost passed out from going into spiritual trance. I have touched other people while shaking and have found this conduct to be respected and valued. After I joined the church, I would come home after service and sit at the piano and a sacred song would come through me. I would then write the lyrics, typically based on the theme of the pastor's sermon. Sometimes songs would be dedicated and given to particular church members. Again, the relationship of music to opening spiritual doors was revealed. It was the music, whether in song or the rhythmicity and melodic form of sincere praying, that helped activate spiritual energy in the church. I learned how several young black women had fallen under the influence of the spirit and run up to the piano in a church service. They proceeded to play spiritual music perfectly, although they had never learned to play.

One woman in the community, now a highly respected professional gospel singer, had dreamed of a large piano keyboard where Jesus showed her what keys to play. When she awakened, she knew how to play. Such reports are not limited to the church. Edgar Cayce once was hypnotized and told he could play the piano. While in trance he went to a piano and played beautiful music. He never had a lesson in his life, yet in an alternative experiential reality, he was an accomplished musician.

Reverend Jerry McAfee, Minister, New Salem Missionary Baptist Church

The experience of someone in such a situation is not that they are making music. Instead, they experience the music playing them. The keyboard is felt as inseparable from the player. The piano keys sometimes seem to move the fingers of the pianist. This same experience is described by master musicians who live for the moments when the music plays them in such a way.

The creation of this music requires the surrendering of an individual's mind to become a part of a larger, more encompassing mind that includes the musical instrument. What is created is a mind of music, a mind that "circularly connects" the musician and instrument as one. The musician gives up using his limited mind to make music and shifts to being played by the mind of music.

I believe music is not only a way of opening spiritual doors but is the communication of the gods. When a song comes through you and your heart is full, it is possible to become one with the song. In this experience one is taken to visionary realms where spiritual contact is heightened. As Drury (Nevill Drury, *The Elements of Shamanism*, Longread: Element Books, 1989, p. 39) put it, "Songs are the songs of the gods and spirits and . . . can help the shaman feel propelled by their energy." The Apache holy man, Geronimo, once said, "As I sing, I go through the air to a holy place where Yusun (the Supreme Being) will give me the power to do wonderful things. I am surrounded by little clouds, and as I go through the air, I change, becoming spirit only."

For the Klamath Indians, the same word is used to signify both spirit and song. Joan Halifax accurately captures the essence of the sacred song (Joan Halifax, *Shamanic Voices: A Survey of Visionary Narratives*, New York: E. P. Dutton, 1979, p. 30): "As the World Tree stands at the center of the vast planes of the cosmos, song stands at the intimate center of the cosmos of the individual. At that moment when the shaman song emerges, when the sacred breath rises up from the depths of the heart, the center is found, and the source of all that is divine has been tapped."

Africa

Nowhere on earth are the sounds of music and rhythm used more to open spiritual doors than in Africa. During the spring of 1991, when I was fully immersed in the sacred music of the African American community, I was invited to be a visiting professor in South Africa. This continent marked another transition in my journey and was politically marked by my visit to Soweto on the day that apartheid was constitutionally abolished. This continent seemed to be the wellspring and source of raw, unprocessed natural spirituality. One morning before going out to a village to visit some traditional healers, I dreamed of a large lion's face staring at me. We were face to face and the eyes were strengthening and assuring, not terrifying and frightening. Only later would I face the significance of this vision.

Accompanying Marian and me on our way to visit the village was a man named Richard who was introduced as a house painter. Richard was quiet during the entire ride. When we arrived, it became clear that not only did he live in the village, but that he was the minister of the church we were to visit. Richard changed out of his work clothes and reappeared wearing a white robe with a blue stripe. He worked in Pretoria, lived overnight during the work week in a hostel outside the city, and had a family in this village. On a future occasion we stopped to visit him in his hostel. The conditions were worse than any prison I've visited and as terrible as those in photographs I've seen of concentration camps. While we were visiting this hostel, a group of police came marching toward us demanding to know who gave us authority to be there. South Africa was embarrassed by the conditions some of their people lived in and I was taking photographs. We were taken to the police jail and detained while he called "the authorities above him." When he discovered we were Americans, he tried to save face by immediately making up the story that we were officials from the World Health Organization investigating tuberculosis. We were released. Richard had to commute between his village, hostel, and jobs in Pretoria without any personal transportation. He and every member of his village had to rely solely on public transportation. The entire community did not have a single car. Internally, they relied on walking and ox-driven carts. Richard, however, had saved his money for over ten years to finally buy a car for the

Author with Richard, healer and spiritual leader of traditional village, South Africa

community. During the month of our visit, he drove it for the first time and immediately had a wreck with an ox. He had no insurance and the cost of repairing the car was estimated at 2,500 Rand dollars. They had no money, just a broken car they had waited a decade to get. When I heard about this, I donated the money given to me from the university, which happened to be 2,500 Rand. I was later told that the church had prayed all night for a miracle to save their car. The money arrived the next morning. Hearing that news was one of the best gifts I have ever received.

Richard's church combined Christian and traditional African spiritual practice and was the center of the community life. They had church every day of the week. Service consisted of scriptural reading, hymns accompanied by the pastor's ringing of a small bell and rapid hand clapping by the congregation, and an opportunity for testimony and prayer from all members including the visitors. The service ended with a healing ceremony where all church members quickly went up front to drink holy water drawn from a bucket and then went under the joined arms of church elders who touched everyone with their free hands.

Following a meal prepared for us by the community, we were taken to a woman sangoma, a traditional African healer. She explained how she used herbs in her practice and how she divined with bones and sticks. It was curious to find one of her divining sticks to be a very exotic item for the village — it was a yellow Lego piece she had found. When her talk was over, I asked her what it meant to have a vision of entering a crocodile's mouth and then to have the vision end with the crocodile's teeth as a necklace around one's neck. She took several deep sighs and said she wanted to speak to me alone. She told me this was a powerful dream of a sangoma. I was to find that crocodile necklace and make it my own. I gave her some tobacco I had taken with me on my vision fast and told her of its significance. I thanked her for her time with us. As we were walking along a dirt path through the village, I suddenly looked at the ground and noticed a small mound of volcanic-like rock that I later discovered was a meteor. I gave an offering and picked up a small piece and placed it in my pocket. Later when I retrieved it to show Marian, she said, "Look at it. It's the face of a lion."

I looked and saw the face that appeared in my morning dream. Two days before, Marian and I had visited the home of Stan, a professor who studied African healing traditions at the University of South Africa. He took me to a special room filled with many masks and various items used in ceremony. I immediately went into trance and was filled with a spirit that seemed connected to one mask in particular. I made sounds and chants I never had heard before.

One hour before going into the room, we had taken an auto trip. While pulled over to the side of the road, I had touched his back with deep vibrations and he had almost passed out. He got out of the car and walked around to gather his wits. He then explained that something had been opened up in him and he felt some energy inside his chest he hadn't felt since he was a child. When we went to Stan's special room later that evening, I went into trance and asked him to lie down on the floor. I worked on him with vibrational massage and chanting. He began making sounds and with time we were spontaneously chanting together, sounding like two baboons singing the same chorus. Here I had the vision of entering the crocodile's mouth. It was my entry to the spirits in that room.

At the end of our work together that evening, I saw a vision of the necklace of crocodile teeth around my neck. Later that same evening I complained to Stan about a pain on the side of my hip. He was quick to tell me that their eight-year-old son had had surgery performed on that part of his body. I took this as a signal for us to work with his son. We invited him into the room and he sat on his daddy's lap. His dad surrounded him with a huge hug, and I began applying my hands to his body. The presence of healing, bonding, and love was thick in the room that evening. When our work was finished, the boy ran out of the room shouting to his mother and Marian, "I've been purified!"

Stan arranged a trip to yet another village, where I was introduced to a highly respected healer named Prince. After meeting with a group of us, I asked to see him alone. He took me to his private room with his medicines and altar. We talked and I began vibrating. With his permission I placed my hands on his heart and back and began to do some work. He described his own pain, which is one I sometimes have. I've later discovered that many healers have this same pain. Prince told me I was a very powerful healer and would spend the rest of my life healing others. He said I had everything I needed except a small piece of understanding, which would soon come. He offered to help me with this and gave me medicines to ingest and smoke to inhale while he performed prayer and ceremony. In the following days, it became clearer to me that perhaps this was what I was supposed to do. Although I was practicing a spiritual lifestyle, I hadn't

Prince, Sangoma in Mamelodi, South Africa

fully accepted what I was doing. It was as if the main part of my life was being lived in secret, a secret to both others and to a part of myself.

The following day, Stan took me into the countryside to a thatch hut. Oddly enough, it was in an almost hidden area next to a nationalistic monument celebrating the founding of South Africa. Without saying a word, he gestured to enter the circular hut. I crawled in and immediately noticed it looked like a sweat lodge. A circular fire pit was in the middle of the barren ground. I laid down and began shaking very violently. My whole body was convulsing and my feet and legs were beating the ground creating the rhythmic sound of a frenzied drum. At times I felt my body spinning.

I then had a vision of a face. It was so vivid that I reached out with my hands and traced its outline. The face was an African healer with a single bone coming out of each side of his cheeks. My arm spontaneously reached into the fire pit and grabbed something from the bottom and I began telling Stan what I saw. He told me to look at what I was holding. It was the bone, the exact bone I was seeing in the face. I then turned around and reached underneath the thatch and pulled out a clay like stone. I picked up something else with my other hand and crumbled it over the fire pit, made a prayer, and left.

After leaving, Stan said it was traditional to crumble clay to create a reddish dust in the way I had done. He then told me that the hut was called the "place of faces." "If you come here and see a face," he went on, "you will then find this person in your future." I also described to him a path and place I saw in my vision. Stan said I would someday find this man. I then told him about the stone and when we looked at it, it appeared as a carving of this man's face.

My last outing with Stan involved the two of us, with Marian and another friend of his, trekking to a mountain outside a village. We climbed to the top with hardly a word uttered. I began to sing and bring forth the sound of what I loved in Native American spirituality. I touched each person, and Stan and I went off to a precipice where we shook and sang together in the voices of the African spirits.

It was approaching darkness and there may have been some concern whether we could get back to our car while there was still light. I became filled with a sense of where to go and literally ran down the mountain along a way that enabled us to be at the car in a matter of minutes. Along the way, I picked up four white stones, one for each of us, each stone having an image of a face.

Marian and I visited other cities in South Africa where I had to lecture. In a shop in Durban, we purchased an incredible Zulu wood carving of a crocodile whose jaws were connected to a man whose face from one angle was a bird, and whose hand reached for the heavens. The carving embodied much of what had happened.

When I was with Stan, I felt compelled to give him a special gift. I had brought with me a Zuni ring, thinking it would be a gift for someone. I also had brought my pipe and other sacred things, which, to our amazement, were never seen in the close inspections we went through at the London airport prior to flying to South Africa.

I felt an urge to give Stan my pipe, but my mind resisted, believing such an object is never to be given up. Instead I gave him the ring. Within a short time of presenting this gift, he dropped it and the stones all fell out and broke into what seemed like hundreds of pieces. It made no sense to onlookers how this could have physically happened. I knew I had given the wrong gift and corrected the situation by giving up my pipe.

Our final week in Africa was a visit to Kruger National Park, a renowned wildlife preserve. We were escorted by a couple, Peter and Ansie, whom we had become very close to, along with their friend, Brian, an ecologist and ranger. In the bush, my dreams at night blurred into the surroundings. I felt I could walk with the animals, embody them, and see what they saw.

The call to heal continued to be heard in the bush. One evening Marian and I performed a healing ceremony with Ansie, who felt creatively blocked. She reported feeling energy go through her head and light shooting out of her fingertips. She made a resolution to take up painting seriously again. Ansie and Peter felt more deeply connected with us that evening. We had joined in some way that would keep us connected as family. Ansie later mailed us a water color painting she had done depicting an African landscape we had witnessed together.

Invitations to Heal

Our trip to Africa in June, 1991 had confirmed beyond a doubt the call to heal. The question remained, however, as to what the proper context for this healing was. Upon returning, I found people coming to me asking for help. I gave a brief explanation of what I do, making it clear it is only used for good purposes, and that it is unique for each person. Somehow, and in some way, each person gets only what they need and not so much as would endanger them. I found people sometimes felt they were taken to the very edge of what they could handle, that if any more energy were exchanged, they would begin to be fearful. I simply trusted the process and found each person received as much as they needed and that it ended when it needed to be stopped.

As we pondered what direction we should follow, one morning, Marian and I went out to a sacred site to spend a day and night fasting and praying. In this prayer fast, I learned the relative unimportance of the sacred objects, stones, and gifts I had received. Indeed, I was beginning to feel proud of "owning" these gifts or "spiritual trophies," and I got a spiritual spanking for it. What should never be forgotten is that all that is necessary for spiritual work is humble, strong prayer and faith. No physical objects are necessary. You are the pipe. You embody the altar.

I went home and disposed of every sacred object, stone, and gift I had except for one item. It was clear I was to be the custodian of the eagle feather passed on to me by the Ojibway medicine man. Everything else went. I was stripped of most of my sacred objects. I turned to prayer alone.

Everything I've learned experientially fits with what I've been told by elder healers — the motor for spiritual development is simply prayer. All the rest is glitter. "Pray hard and pray harder" is the best advice to give to someone who is spiritually hungry.

There are many ways to pray. Many different words, requests, offerings, and sounds may be used. One may shout or be quiet. One may be intelligible or unintelligible. One may pray for a blade of grass or an entire ecosystem. One may moan, groan, cry, laugh, jump with joy, or beg for pity. Conventional recipes for prayer conduct are dangerous when people use them to restrict other possibilities and forms for communing with spirit. Experiment with prayers. Make them a laboratory for spiritual discovery.

Many of the most powerful spiritual encounters I've had have been with the image of Jesus. He is the oldest spiritual image in my life, having grown up in a Baptist preacher's household. Both my father and grandfather were preachers and I was raised in the country church of a small Midwestern farm community. I can still remember the current that drew me forward as a child attending a revival meeting in my father's church. It is one of my earliest spiritual experiences.

In my adult life I have seen visions of Jesus on the cross and I have hung with Him. I have awakened in the night to find myself holding His hands and feeling an electric-like current charging throughout my body. I usually have had to let go of His hands or pass out from the intensity of the connection. He has handed me a glass of white light that I have drunk, filling my insides with warm energy.

One day in the fall of 1991, I awakened early in the morning and found myself in a celestial church. I was asked to talk and did not know what to say. The only words that came to help me were the words said over and over by my minister, Reverend McAfee, "Let it come from the heart."

I knew ego, pride, and self stood in the way. I shouted out as loud as I could to this self, "Get off me!" I then saw a thin, white film that had been wrapped around my heart come off and float away. At that moment, Jesus appeared and covered me with a robe to cover my spiritual nakedness. Words then began to flow:

"Oh precious Lord Jesus, we call upon you to open and touch our hearts and receive your spirit. We ask that you remove all constraints and closed doors that interfere with our meeting you. Cast away all barriers and concerns for ourselves and deliver us unto your arms. We know we cannot fully know you unless we are ready to die right now, this very moment in this very prayer. Hear our surrender now. Take our minds and wed them with thine."

In this celestial church, I went on preaching to the congregation:

"Faith is never enough. Faith must be acted upon. Jesus did not say, 'follow me after you study and pass an examination.' He didn't say, 'follow me when you understand me.' He didn't say, 'follow me because you are ready.' He didn't say, 'follow me because you are worthy.' He said, 'Follow me.'

"His call is to stand up and take a step without the benefit of totally understanding what you are doing. His call is to feed the hungry even when you don't understand how you can. His call is to heal the sick even when you don't think you know how. His call is to walk with Him even though you don't know where the journey will take you.

"And so I ask you to act in His faith. Stand up and let Him speak. Stand up and let Him feed the hungry. Stand up and let Him heal the troubled. Stand up and listen to where He wants to carry you."

The celestial service ended with the choir singing the gospel music I had grown accustomed to hearing at New Salem.

Several weeks later, I was startled in the middle of the night by a voice describing itself as the "voice of God." I was invited to give my life to healing and was told I would be shown the face of God. I was taken toward the edge of a high mountain in a fog of white light where I faced huge, pointed masses of stone rising into the sky, looking something like upside down glaciers. The area was bathed in white light, making it impossible to see the edge. As I got closer, the light was brighter and I could see less. God was raw strength and energy with a calm sense of neutrality toward all things.

Sometimes my dreams of Jesus have been mixed with other spiritual traditions. I have seen Him hold out His arms to show that inside His robe were all the birds and creatures of the earth. It was a message that these other spirits are not in conflict with Him. They all belong to the same kingdom.

In another dream during the fall of 1991, I met a medicine man who had my face. He took me to a waterfall and said to jump off. He reminded me of a lesson I had learned a long time before, in 1976 when, under hypnosis, I was told to re-experience my birth. At that time, I saw my birth as being from an old propeller driven airplane with a rough hole in its side where people lined up to jump out. When it became my turn, I looked out the hole and saw many, many search lights in the sky moving in different directions. It was a night sky filled with fog. I realized that the purpose of birth and of life itself was to squint and concentrate in such a fashion that all these beams of light would align themselves as one light line. One was then to jump following this line down to earth.

Fifteen years later, I dreamed of being told by a medicine man to use this technique to jump off a waterfall. He said I would be able to stop my flight midway in the fall and find a cloud of white light within which I would find a place to sit. In that light, Jesus would appear and be present to help. I was told I could use this in my work with healing others.

William Tall Bull
and the Great Medicine Wheel

Our trip to Africa in June of 1991 and the subsequent healing work did not finally resolve my struggle with how to contextualize this practice. Three months after our trip, I dreamed of William Tall Bull, a medicine man I had met six months earlier at a conference on Native American Culture. As the lead medicine man of the Cheyenne, he had been invited to speak on traditional medicine. I went to this conference and, upon arrival, discovered his speech had been moved to the last hour. After sitting through several angry protest talks, it was finally time for the last talk. William Tall Bull took the stage, appearing as an old man with a slumped presence who began telling simple stories. People in the crowd for some reason were fidgeting and making noise and many left. In the end, there was a small, quiet group of us, eager to hear his voice.

William Tall Bull spoke of how his people's medicine is learned. He told the story of a man who returned from a hunt to discover that his people had moved. As was the custom, markings were given enabling him to find them. He did not go on, however, because he found an old lame dog left behind. The dog had injured his leg and was in pain. This man decided to stay and attempt to nurse the dog back to health. He patiently comforted and cared for the dog. One night, while asleep by the fire, the man had a dream in which the dog came to him and spoke. The dog thanked him for the care he had received and said, "In the morning when you wake up, you will find me dead by your side. As an expression of my gratitude, I will give you a gift. When you awaken you are to remove my eyelids and place them in a pouch to be worn around your neck. When people come to you requesting that their eyes be healed, you are to aim the pouch toward their eyes." From that day on, the man became a medicine man specializing in healing eyes, particularly snow blindness. When he aimed the pouch toward people's eyes, what looked like streams of white crystals could be seen going from the pouch to the eyes. The dog had given the man the gift of healing.

After William Tall Bull's talk, I went up to him and told him how much I was moved by his words. I asked if it would be possible to visit him in the future and he stared into my eyes and said, "You bet." Half a year later I dreamed of William Tall Bull. The very same day I took my son to a newsstand to get some baseball cards and noticed a new magazine on Native American culture. I opened it up and there was a photograph of William Tall Bull. I knew I had to see him.

I went to my office and tried to call him. He had no phone. I then called the local college, Dullknife Community College in Lamedeer, Montana, and they said he would be stopping by in an hour. We connected by phone and I told him about my dream of him and a medicine wheel. He said for the first time in their history, different medicine men from many different Indian nations were meeting to discuss the spiritual preservation of the Great Medicine Wheel. He said the meeting would take place in two days at Crow Agency and invited me to see him there.

Marian and I took off the next morning. It was an eighteen hour drive to the Wyoming-Montana area. On the way I kept seeing the medicine wheel in my mind. It became an obsession, like the scene in *Close Encounters of the Third Kind* where people can't stop thinking about Devil's Tower. I didn't know anything about the medicine wheel other than that anthropologists had hypothesized its possible function as a calendar.

As I drove the car, I observed something that wasn't exactly a dream or a vision. I experienced an "inner seeing" of the medicine wheel. In this inner seeing I encountered the wheel as a sacred place for spiritual travel and vision. I saw a medicine person sitting in one of the small circles to assume the voice for songs the spirits wanted to sing. In another small circle, an initiate sat with a small spirit Indian. The markings on the stones were not of a flat, two-dimensional calendar or clock but were the two-dimensional representation of a three dimensional structure. Specifically, I saw a large spirit tepee, where each stone was the marking of the base of a spirit pole that intersected in tepee fashion with the other poles.

The center of the circle was an altar marked by a stone with orange coloring to be used as a pillow for one's head. I was witnessing a sacred ceremony, where the spirits sing through the voice of the medicine man, while the small, short, spirit Indian carries the initiate into a spirit journey. They go under the earth through a vortex below the small circle space, moving through pathways of other vortices. The initiate is taken whirling and whirling through and out of the earth. The ceremony reaches its climax when the initiate moves to the center of the large circle, lays his head on the altar stone, and weeps for a vision to guide him.

As we drove, I kept seeing the color "orange" associated with this medicine wheel and told Marian, "If I see orange there, I'm going to kiss the ground." We drove straight to the great wheel. The mountains surrounding the entrance to this sacred site bring out some of the strongest spiritual presences I've ever felt associated with a place. As we made the final ascension to the site and began walking to it, the first thing I saw was the color orange. It was on the stone near the center. It was present everywhere, both on the stones and on the Indian offerings and sacred objects. I wept and kissed the ground that held the Great Medicine Wheel. We offered tobacco, gave prayers, and set out to find Tall Bull.

Crow Agency, we soon discovered, was celebrating its annual Crow fair. Several hundreds maybe even a thousand, tepees were set up, and horses were everywhere. One could get a glimpse of what it used to be like. In looking for Tall Bull, we were introduced to John Hill, the head medicine man of the Crow. I told him I had had a dream but did not mention the details, and he smiled, saying, "You've been initiated. It happens to people from all over the world. People have been called to the medicine wheel in their dreams and have come from as far away as Germany and Japan." He welcomed us with his humor and graciousness.

We attended the meeting that evening and the next morning. It largely focused on a New York lawyer trying to help the elders use legal methods to protect their sacred sites from tourism and land development. I remained still until I felt unable to stop the words from coming out of my mouth. I asked for permission to speak, and, when given the opportunity, I reminded them that although lawyers were fine, it should never be forgotten that spiritual crises are best solved through spiritual solutions. I said that turning to their own sacred ways and ceremonies should not be forgotten in all of the debates over politics, treaties, and laws. Several elders indicated their approval. One, in particular, Francis Brown, an elder of the Arapahoe, gave me his name and phone number, saying he was available if I ever needed any spiritual help.

My meeting with William Tall Bull was scheduled for the next day at noon. When we met, I told him my story and laid my hands on him. He said his uncle healed with his hands and went on to tell me some things, including a way of preparing a bear powder medicine. It involved collecting the ash of a particular tree and placing it in a pouch to be worn around the neck. Although he told me what this medicine was for, I don't know why he told it to me, but I have remembered it for the future. He also told me the spirits would soon give me a name. He indicated he knew what I was talking about when I described the ritual of the medicine wheel and said he secretly visits the Great Medicine Wheel after dark when the rangers aren't around. He said it was available for me to use, although he said its power could be summoned from anywhere in that area.

He also shared with me two important lessons he had learned. First he said that things got better for his community when he became quieter and spent more time in the woods away from people. This move into quiet had done the most to help his community. Second, he said, "All these medicines we use aren't what they seem. It's *belief* that is the strongest medicine." People, in other words, sometimes need a little lever, prop, or medicine to help activate their belief.

He told me the visions he had experienced in his life. One of his past relatives, a historically important medicine man, had spoken to him as a spirit and passed on to him the spiritual leadership of many Indian people. I thanked him for his words and said I would go back home.

More Lessons and Dreams

As we were leaving, another medicine man, who seemed less connected to the others, asked for a ride. We agreed and during the trip we all exchanged stories. He was a "heyoka" or "contrary" who, for sacred reasons does things backwards. Heyokas, among the Lakota people, act as sacred clowns to help keep the community balanced. He invited us to his house to sweat and we accepted. What took place that evening was undoubtedly one of the strangest events of our lives.

First of all, turning onto a side road and entering the heart of the Badlands at sunset is a scene straight out of a science fiction movie. The place is other-worldly, reminding one of the moon's surface. When we finally got to his house, deeply isolated from civilization, he showed us his lodge and altar and we began making preparations for the sweat. What seemed a bit unusual was the way he heated the stones. He poured an enormous amount of gasoline and threw a match. An eighteen foot high flame burst forth. I was accustomed to heating the stones in the more traditional and more time consuming manner. When the rocks were ready and the altar set, we entered the lodge.

Following his prayers and ritual, he turned to us to pray. After a while, the medicine man said, "Open er' up." I immediately went into deep chanting. He then shouted, "Open 'er up!" I reached even more deeply and really "Opened 'er up" with a thunderous chant. He began to shout again and again, "Open 'er up!" I thought, "I've never been pushed to go for it this way, but let's open 'er up." I began chanting and speaking like something from another world. He then threw the bucket of water on me and my first thought was, "My God, this is incredible. It's like getting whacked on the head by the stick of a Zen master. This guy's really pushing me to the max. Maybe he's trying to help push me into another dimension." So up a notch I went and my voice became the voice of thunder.

By this time he opened the entry flap and demanded we get out. He seemed afraid and began asking what language we had spoken. He said someone had called him by his spirit name. The man was clearly rattled and my survival response was not to do anything that would escalate his fear.

The whole spiritual fiasco had been brought about by a simple miscommunication. When he said "Open 'er up," he meant open up the flap or door to the lodge, letting in some cool air. We thought he meant get deeper into our praying. It did amaze us that we had called out his spirit name.

We sat quietly while he lectured us on various evils. He became very authoritative, nonloving, and nonspiritual. We simply let him speak, thanked him, dressed, and left. We were in the car in the middle of the Badlands in pitch dark at midnight and for several minutes we didn't talk. I slowed the car down, turned to Marian, and said, "That was absolutely insane!" We laughed with relief. The situation had been totally absurd, an episode from the theatre of the ridiculous. We replayed it over and over as if it were a play designed to expose how crazy it gets when one tiny misunderstanding escalates into an uncontrollable runaway. We were glad to finally get back on the main road again. We thought we had learned how important it is to develop an ability to discern when *not* to be open. We never once considered that a pure heyoka might say the opposite of what he means.

When we returned home, I received a copy of Richard Katz's book, *Boiling Energy*. It is an account of healing among the Kalahari Kung or

Bushmen in Africa. The book had a major impact on me. As presented in this book, the Kalahari Bushmen seemed to possess a spiritual practice closer to what I was experiencing than any other I had encountered.

These people regularly perform healing dances around a fire, which helps arouse an energy in them they call "Num." Healers experience this energy boiling in their guts and then moving up into their head, resulting in body shaking and trance experience. They then touch and hold and vibrate other community members as part of the healing process. I was immediately drawn to meet these people and believed I should go to Africa again.

I also felt a strong urge to call Francis Brown, the Arapahoe elder I had met at Crow Agency. He had offered his help at that time and I had often thought of calling him. I was partly interested in talking with him because of the Arapahoe's historical association with the Ghost Dance. The Ghost Dance took place around the turn of the century and spread across many Indian nations, ending in the massacre at Wounded Knee where Indians were slaughtered by the U. S. military for dancing it.

It is somewhat similar, in my opinion, to the healing dance of the Kalahari Bushmen. The Ghost Dancers would dance, have "involuntary trembling," "violent spasmodic movements," and fall into a "final death-like unconsciousness" where communication with the departed took place (James Mooney, *The Ghost Dance Religion and Wounded Knee*, New York: Dover, 1973, p.924). Sometimes prayer involved placing their hands on others' heads in a manner similar to the laying on of hands in the Christian church.

Francis Brown is responsible for seeing that the traditional ceremonies of his people are carried out as traditionally prescribed. When I reached him he quickly suggested I see a Yuwipi man, a medicine man who brings forth the spirits in a very holy ceremony. He offered to inquire in South Dakota as to what Yuwipi man might be available. He suggested I get back in touch with him to make the necessary arrangements.

Several months later, I dreamed about a feather with a particular design on it and its association with three colored sticks. For some reason, I felt drawn to visit the local zoo. I assumed it had to do with looking for that feather. Due to the cold January weather no one was outside at the zoo. I basically had the place to myself. While there I encountered three buffalo. The power of this animal is almost too great to be borne. Respecting its presence, I did not make direct contact at first. The male was face to face with me. After I had been singing for a while, the female got off the ground and came to me. The bull walked away. When the female came, we looked eye to eye. It felt like she would drown me. I knew I would see that buffalo in my dreams.

Listen to the Spirits

I am well aware of how absurd and ridiculous it sometimes is to talk about shamanic or spiritual experiences within the context of the standard view of Western understanding and culture. However, I don't always view this difference of "knowing ways" to be a problem. Sometimes it is a resourceful advantage. A heavy dose of shamanic imagination can be balanced by laughing at how ridiculous it looks through the everyday standard view. This can help dissipate any excessive heaviness associated with shamanic work.

On the other hand, I am also aware of traveling between two worlds. In a shamanic context, visions, prophecies, healing touch, celestial concerts, astral travel, and so on seem natural and normal. Here the rest of the everyday world is seen as blind, deaf, and ignorant. Nevertheless, unless one moves to a reservation, the Amazon jungle, Siberia, Fiji, or the Kalahari, to name a few exceptions, one is faced with the politics of managing the entries and exits of talking with others about these worlds of experience.

My own personal history has been as much an effort to escape the call of a shamanic walk as it has been to seek it. I have purposefully stayed away from teachers, gurus, institutes, institutions, and ashrams. I have many times sincerely walked away from all of this, believing I would never be open to another shamanic experience. It didn't matter because something would happen to me independent of my intentions. It wouldn't leave me alone. I was forced to be tormented by it or learn to live with it. I have chosen to follow my dreams, visions, and the voice I hear within me. I once asked William Tall Bull whether it was important to work within the rules, constraints, and discipline of a particular tradition. He said, "Don't worry about it, just listen to what the spirits tell you."

I have been through several existential crises trying to understand how I was "supposed to" fit what I did into other spiritual traditions. In Louisiana, I was taken to the home of a self-described "Christian healer" who told me that contact with any source of spirit outside (his) definitions of biblical scripture was a sure sign of evil. I did not immediately dismiss his words but tried to learn and benefit what I could from the questions and challenges he presented. I prayed to be led to what was good and right in my work. Repeatedly, I acknowledged in my prayers that I am willing to turn away from this walk if it is not a healing service to others. Time and time again, I would set out the rationally generated questions: Is my shamanic life to be organized and constrained by the teachings of Christianity? Am I to abandon Christianity and move singularly to a form of Native American spiritual understanding? Should I move to Africa? . . . The more I thought, the more questions I generated, and the more confused and intellectually constipated I became.

When I would get away from it all and just sit, waiting for an answer, I would always come back to the same understanding: Listen to what the spirits tell you. I have come to accept that the world's various "churchologies," whether Christian, Native American, Muslim, Buddhist or whatever, specify rather arbitrary prescriptions that are largely independent of the way the spiritual world works. To paraphrase Jung, many churches seem to exist to make it impossible for anyone to have a spiritual experience. One must follow the voice that comes to one. Only through prayer and harder prayer and uncompromising sincerity can one be sure that one is doing all that one can do to assure the goodness of one's intentions. And only through dialogue and participation in communities of other people and creatures can one's walk be further tuned to best fit the natural ecology.

Some visions don't make sense to me at the time and it's only later that their meaning begins to emerge. Some are seeds for other harvests. I once was shown a white, trumpeted plant. I entered it and traveled down it's root. Near the end of the root, a filament was bounded by white light. In my dream I removed this filament from the root and ingested it. For several days I looked in books for this plant and discovered it was the morning glory, a plant whose seeds had been taken for sacred purposes by the Mayans.

I was once startled by a dream so real I had to check my body to see if it was taking place. I was seeing a tree grow out of my body. I saw the trunk coming right out of the flesh. In these ways, my life is led by the guides and signposts of the spiritual world. Sometimes I'm told to make something or go find someone. In being obedient to these directions, the journey moves forward.

I accept the many different forms of spiritual practice as analogous to the different styles of music or genres of literature. I will not limit myself to listening to any particular style of music because of some general rule dictated by someone else (Roberto Assagioli, the founder of psychosynthesis, once warned people about listening to jazz). In a similar vein, I will go in the doors of cathedrals, churches, synagogues, temples, and lodges, among other places, whenever the spirits call.

As I was coming to peace with being fully open to walking this shamanic path, I had a dream where my family of origin and those closest to me were in the living room of a medicine man's home. After some social conversation, he took me back to a private room and asked some questions to see what I was familiar with. After recognizing all he was talking about, he said, "There's no more I can teach you. You are now on your own." Medicine people and teachers can take you into the world of spirit. Once you are there, the spirits take over the teaching job.

The Call of the Kalahari

While realizing the call to return to Africa, I began challenging myself as to why I should go. I recognized that I didn't really know. I did believe the Kalahari Bushmen were practicing a way of healing that was close to what I had developed without any instruction from or awareness of them. My desire was simply to be with them. It felt like a call to come home.

The question of how to reconcile my connection to diverse, and what some would consider conflicting, sources of spirit continued to worry me. I might be "possessed" by powerful spirits in Africa or "possessed" by

Jesus. I resolved this conflict by asking God to protect me from anything that was not good, and I, in turn, would get out of the way and let the spirits come through. This removed the burden of having to judge, evaluate, and discern every spiritual knock. I simple handed it over to the Great One I had no doubts about.

In prayer, I began to understand more clearly that the call to the Kalahari was to encounter directly the healing dance of the Bushmen. I began to wonder whether I would be conducting these dances as part of my own work. I was also clear that I was to communicate this directly to the Bushmen and ask for their blessing and guidance.

In the Kung Bushmen healing dance, some of the healers enter an experiential realm they regard as "death." Here "the fear and pain of that boiling num, the terror of that passage, is faced and overcome as individuals die to themselves. From the death of the individual Kung personality, the rebirth of the Kung healer must come." (Katz, p.134). Opening and entering spiritual worlds requires experiencing the death of one's previously stabilized identity. This is the case for all spiritual traditions and occurs over and over in the life of a healer.

My grandfather struggled to ignore the call of being a preacher. When he was a young man with a wife and five-year-old son, there was a revival meeting in town and he refused to go. Finally, his family got him to go one night and reluctantly he went, wearing old boots and work clothes. The next night he woke up in the middle of the night sobbing and crying out loud. It awakened everyone in the house. He had experienced a spiritual encounter so intense that he never shared the specifics of it to anyone throughout his life. What he did say was simply, "I'm just going to have to preach."

His five-year-old son, my dad, ran into the bedroom and said, "Mother, is daddy going to die?" She calmed him, and the next evening at the revival meeting my grandfather put on his best suit and made a public "surrender" to preach, as they called it. The minister preached a sermon about how the son had come into the room asking about whether his daddy had died. The lesson was that he had in fact died and was being born into another life.

These deaths that lead to births into spiritual realms shake our heart and soul. They are sometimes frightening and overwhelming. At every healing dance, the healers face the possibility of dying this death. Years of experiencing it still does not help alleviate the intensity of their concern for the ordeal. Similarly, a sweat provides an opportunity to die, as does a vision fast, or a truly sincere and hard prayer session. All spiritual paths pass through these occasions of dying and becoming reborn. This recycling of one's own life is the highest process of healing for the healer. I agree with Edgar Cayce's suggestion that the "symbology of the crucifixion" is the voluntary relinquishing of the ego or self where what dies is the will of self and what is reborn is the desire to exercise the will of God.

The Spiritual Tepee

The Arapahoe elder Francis Brown had recommended that I visit the Yuwipi man Gary Holy Bull before organizing my second trip to Africa. In February, 1992, I made contact with Gary, who lives in Sisseton, South Dakota. He asked me to make arrangements to visit him for three days. He said to bring tobacco and the four colors of cloth — red, black, white, and yellow.

The very next morning, after talking with Gary Holy Bull I was awakened at 4:00 a.m. to conduct my prayers. This particular morning I was extremely focused. Only once did I drift and, when I did, I heard a very loud, high-pitched sound — almost a combination of an eagle's cry and a bark. It jolted me and I remained focused for the remaining time.

Following my prayer, a voice and vision gave me specific directions as to what I was to do with the sticks I had dreamed about several months before. I was both "shown" and told to get three different sticks from the woods, all being the same height as me. One was to be found in the west and would be dark in color, another in the east that would be red, and a yellowish one from the south. Each stick was to be shaved to a point on the top end and an angle cut on the bottom. I was told that further instruction would be given in the future as to the carvings each stick would receive.

The sticks were to be connected at the tops by strips of leather wound in a particular way. Each was to be placed in its appropriate position, east, south, and west. The north position was to be kept open. I was told that I was to be that stick. With my white skin, I represented the north. I was not to stand, but to lie down with my head in the center of this arrangement of sticks. Hanging by a string in the middle of this set up was a feather with a particular design on it. It was to hang just above my head.

While smoking my pipe that morning, I was drawn to hold the eagle feather given to me on my first vision fast. While holding it, I saw that it was the feather I had been looking for. The design I had seen in my vision was on it. I had looked everywhere and had given up, only to find it was the feather I had all along. The feather became empowered in a way I had not realized before. I began using it to help guide my spiritual work.

In this configuration of sticks, I was aware that each direction and color represented the four major spiritual cultures. In my vision I was also shown sacred animals associated with each stick. The west was accessed by a spirit bear, the east with the eagle, and the south with a wolf. The presence of the buffalo embraced and pervaded all the directions. As I prayed and addressed these directions, I received a song and chant from each spirit animal. With the vision of this spiritual tool, I was beginning to understand how the many different aspects of my spiritual practice were coming together. Previous differences were now becoming parts of a more embracing unity. The purity and clarity of this vision moved me deeply and represented a new development in my spiritual life.

As the time grew nearer for my visit to Gary Holy Bull, I prayed harder every morning, often from two to three hours. I have learned to let my prayers move naturally. Sometimes one needs to sing or make sounds; at other times one needs just to be in silence. Responding to the call at the moment gives one energy and life. One's prayer will then move on its own. Trying to say a memorized prayer or use a template for praying requires will power and will power will tire and short-out very rapidly!

Prayer is a time for calibrating and tuning our relations with all our relatives. Acknowledging all directions, all creatures, all forms of being, and all ways of expression places us correctly in the Grand Station for all Living Things. From the African American church and the Native Americans, I learned to pray with all my heart and being. They taught me that prayer will lead the one praying, not the other way around.

A Spiritual Explosion at New Salem Missionary Baptist Church

The week before I met Gary Holy Bull, an unusual event took place at New Salem. On the morning before this particular church service, I prayed very hard to receive direction as to whether the spirits were calling me to remain there. I immediately had a vision of being in the church with the spirits working very actively. That very morning the church witnessed the most intense manifestation of the Holy Spirit in its entire history.

When the worship service began, one could feel electricity in the air. I turned to Marian and said, "This is high voltage." For whatever reason, the largest crowd ever had gathered in the church that day, and deacons and many men had to sit outside the sanctuary to allow people in. It was the most packed assembly of human beings I had ever been in. When the choir sang, they were solid, tight, and very similar to the celestial choir I sometimes hear in my morning prayers. Everyone could feel the energy cooking.

I began vibrating in a very deep way and singing the songs at the top of my lungs. And then the Holy Spirit began to enter the people. To the best of my memory, it began with a woman whose cries of Hallelujah turned into cries of laughter and ecstasy. I then made eye contact with the minister. We each knew that the other had been "holding back" in church.

I was now aware of having shifted into a deep spiritual place where there is no fear of embarrassment or cautiousness. I was directly tuned into the Holy Spirit, (I had, in fact, been praying for three hours before the service) and had a sense of absolute certainty that I could get out of the way and let the Holy Spirit do its work. This sense of certainty was visible on my face and was actually seen by the minister as we exchanged glances and we both jerked and shook. Then I let go, really let go, and then it began happening in the middle of the church service. My whole body was shaking with my arms and hands violently trembling. I sometimes jumped, shouted, moaned, danced, and vibrated in every possible way. At times I would reach my shaking arms and hands to the heavens and my whole body would move as if it were a snake.

At the same time the church began to explode with the Holy Spirit. Most members of the choir were wailing and passing out. Throughout the church people were jumping, crying, and showing diverse forms of spirit manifestation. Deacons were carrying out members who had been overwhelmed by the spirit. I was so worked up that Marian and two church ushers were fanning me and placing wet towels on my face. I sometimes thought I was in the vision I had had earlier that morning.

The dance of the Holy Spirit kept up for the whole service. The energy was flying in every corner of the sanctuary. The minister abandoned his sermon and let the Holy Spirit do its work. At the end he called for those who wanted healing to come forth. One by one he layed his hands on those who came, and prayers were offered throughout the church. The church deacons were also laying hands and praying. When I went to the minister, he laid his hands on me and began speaking in tongues. My whole body began shaking and I collapsed to the floor. When I got up, I was in such a deep state of ecstasy that I went around hugging, touching, shaking, and vibrating all those I felt drawn to.

The service was nearly three hours in duration. When it was over, no one could believe it. It felt like a dream. People throughout the day would say, "Do you believe what happened?" The minister said he had never witnessed anything like it, and news spread throughout the community about the service. Even to this moment I can not remember everything that happened. Parts of the service aren't available to my memory. It was spiritual dream-time.

Meeting Gary Holy Bull

When I drove to South Dakota on March 23, 1992 to meet Gary Holy Bull, I reflected on the sacred meaning of the different directions and the manifestation of Wakan Tanka, or Great Spirit, through all living things. It set me in the right frame of mind to meet Holy Bull. We met at his house, eighteen miles outside Sisseton, South Dakota. His home and sweat lodge overlook two lakes and a wooded area.

When Gary and I met, we exchanged stories. I spoke sincerely of the experiences that had happened to me and told him I really wasn't sure why I had come. His first words to me were, "I've been waiting for you since I was sixteen years old. My father told me about you at that time." He went on to say that his father had visited him in the sweat lodge two nights before as a spirit and told him that I was the man he had been waiting to meet. His father, as a spirit, showed Gary my face. He recognized me the second we met.

Gary Holy Bull said the world as we know it is changing and its very survival is threatened. His father told him that a time would come when four people would meet and go to a special place and make a prayer. He told him they would represent the four different colors of skin. Gary said that he and I needed to sweat and pray and find out what we were supposed to do.

Gary, his wife, Rita, and their children live in the old ways. They often sweat and pray together with their friends and relatives. He looks over the annual sun dance at Sisseton and elsewhere, conducts Yuwipi ceremonies in his home, and travels throughout the country.

Gary had been part of a group of Indians that went to Libya to accept a peace prize from Kaddafi. Libya awards its own peace prizes and several hundred nations, mostly third world countries, participate. Libya does not recognize the United States as a country but recognizes Indian nations as the true holders of this land. Both the United States and Italy did all they could to detain these North American Indians from traveling to Libya to receive the award. They were held up in New York City for several days and then were harassed in Italy. In Rome, part of the airport was evacuated to detain the small group of North American Indians. Throughout the night, Italian soldiers with uzis aimed their guns at them and pulled triggers so clicks could be heard. Gary's wife, Rita, and some of the other women burst into tears with fright.

They endured the torturous ordeal and finally arrived in Libya where they were treated as heroes. Whatever they wanted they received with excessive generosity. They once asked for a bottle of pop and a whole case arrived. Feasts were given, and they were taken into the mountains to be welcomed by secret forces. They were even introduced to the suicide squads whose feast included grabbing live chickens and eating them raw. Gary said that particular experience was too much to handle.

Gary and I talked for several days, and we participated in sweat lodge ceremonies every evening. We discovered we were the same age and that

Gary Holy Bull

both our careers focused on working with families. He had struggled with local proponents of current psychological and medical models for years, trying to get them to focus on healing families instead of isolated individuals. Gary and Rita's home was open every day to school children, particularly adolescents. He said they sometimes had as many as forty-five children show up in their basement. They teach them the old ways, from dancing and drumming to sewing traditional costumes.

The first sweat with Gary was extremely hot. The stones had heated for nearly four hours and were red hot and large. Some of the people inside the lodge said it felt like a sweat for a Sun Dance. The heat seemed to stretch my face and alter me in a way I hadn't felt before. Staring into the darkness, it opened up into being the whole sky, the entire universe. At times I could see a warm, glowing light in the right periphery of my field of vision. We all prayed hard and I felt profoundly closer to Gary and his family. Some of the men, veterans of many Sun Dances, were somewhat uncomfortable with the presence of a white man. This was a burden for me and made the sweat heavier than it might have been. I felt absolutely exhausted afterwards and struggled in my mind as to what the spirits wanted from me. The burden of this walk felt very heavy and I wasn't sure I could endure. I wished my life were normal. I had been struggling with how to fit into an African American church and now was struggling with how to be connected with the Sisseton Wahpeton Sioux tribe in northeastern South Dakota. At the same time I was soon to head for the Kalahari Desert of Africa and then on to South America and Tokyo. I went to bed with a great need for further prayer but was too weak to pray. I simply asked the spirits for clear direction and fell asleep.

The next morning I awoke overwhelmed with trying to figure out how I was to continue. I wished again I could be free of the many spiritual calls coming my way. Yet my body was now rested and I knew it was possible to survive the walk. My mind was still over-burdened from trying to figure things out, so I continued praying for direction and for the ability to take one small step at a time.

On my way to Gary Holy Bull's house, I stopped at an art museum called the Tekatwitha Fine Arts Center and met the curator, Harold Moore. He and his wife Margery had lived in Rosebud for many years where he was director of the St. Francis Buchel Memorial Lakota Museum. He told me a story about Grey Owl, a man who had been an elder in the Presbyterian church, a deacon in the Catholic church, a member of several other churches, and a practitioner of the old Indian ways. When asked why he practiced so many faiths, he said, "Would you want to get caught in the woods confronting a bear with your pants down?" The humor of the story

camouflages the more profound truth that Native American spiritual practitioners may also be led to making connections with diverse spiritual
traditions.

In preparation for the next night's sweat, Gary and I shared stories about
our past. I touched him with my hands and showed him how I used
vibratory movements for healing. That evening Gary said we would find
out what we were to do. The sweat was even hotter than the night before.
The sweat immediately cleansed me and I found myself not fighting the
heat. I completely surrendered to the breath of the sacred grandfathers and
when it was my turn to pray, I spoke from the deepest part of my heart.
My prayer went something like this:

*"Oh Grandfather, please take pity on me. I sincerely ask you to have pity.
Last night I came to you and my mind knew I was nothing, but you taught
me that my body and heart were also nothing. I learned how pitiful and weak
I really am. Last night and this morning I was too weak to pray strongly.
I could only pray to be helped to walk one step at a time. I know I am not
worthy and am pitiful in front of you.*

*"I am not worthy to be in this sacred place with these good people. I am
thankful they have opened their most sacred place, but I am not worthy. I
know the color of my skin is white and that my people have committed
atrocious acts against these people. I fully face the horror of these acts and
feel ashamed and am further unworthy. I ask you to help correct the ways
of my people. Help me to have the strength to take another step on the good
road. It is so very hard and I am so very weak. Please take pity on me,
Grandfather. Please take pity."*

At this time all the Indians in the sweat lodge began singing a sacred
song as I prayed. My voice and heart became stronger and I shouted and
chanted the rest of my prayer.

*"Oh Grandfather, I am not worthy, but I ask that you watch over my son.
He is an innocent child and I ask that you protect him."*

Before I had begun praying, a stray dog came to the door of the sweat
lodge. No one had seen the dog before, but it was very sick. The dog was
brought in for healing. My heart reached out to the dog and I continued
praying as all the people sang on.

*"Oh Grandfather, I ask that you help me do no harm to any of my
relatives. Teach me to be respectful and loving to all the plants, the grasses
that dance freely in the wind, and the great trees. I acknowledge their wisdom
and teaching and know they are no less than me.*

*"Oh Grandfather, they are even more worthy than I to be heard by you.
I pray for the four leggeds and acknowledge their teachings. I am thankful
for all I have been taught, especially by the wingeds.*

"Oh Grandfather, I confess that I am less worthy than this poor sick dog who has come here tonight. Please heal this dog before you consider me. Make me secondary to this dog who is more worthy. I am thankful for what has been shown to me even though it confuses me. Help me have the understanding that will enable me to be good to all my relatives. I offer my life to you. Please direct me to serve others. I am pitiful and know I am nothing. Please remove all selfishness and self-interest from me. Make me clean and make me pure. I give myself to you, Grandfather. I ask that you have pity and hear my voice. I ask that you hear my voice. I ask these things for all my relatives."

When I stopped, the singing ended and I found my body shaking. I had completely forgotten about the heat and felt very clean and pure. In the final round of the sweat, I opened my eyes and looked up. The heat was the hottest I had ever faced and, afterwards, several Sun Dancers said they almost passed out. In this heat, I asked to die. I felt a release from any concern for the heat and my spiritual eyes were opened. In the dark sky within the lodge, I saw a white skull of a buffalo over the top of the dome just slightly to the west of the center. I then saw a white profile of a very tiny face. When I examined it more carefully, I saw it was my face. It was near the top of the dome just slightly to the east of the center. And then I saw, underneath where the buffalo skull had been, the skull of a dog. It was just above the sacred stones, just west of the center. In this lodge I also felt the presence of the great winged one. I later found out that the great winged one had flown over the lodge during my prayer.

When the sweat was over, everyone praised what a great sweat it had been. I told Gary that I thought I had seen something, and he said we would discuss it after everyone left. We then went to an enormous feast feeling very close like a family. When everyone finally left for the evening, I sat down with Gary and Rita and told them what I thought I had seen. I asked what it meant. Gary said the buffalo skull was their sacred altar and the dog skull was the medicine his people use. The presence of the great winged one was showing me where I would go when I died. He said the eagle was not created, it was always here and would take us one day to where it lives.

Gary said, "You have been blessed with special gifts for seeing and healing. Your call is to heal in the way of Jesus. You are to be a healer for the people in your culture. It will be difficult, and many will give you a hard time because, since the time of Jesus, Christianity has been about creating organizations. It has forgotten His way. We, too, in our own culture have had several people like Jesus. The way you heal is the way He healed. That is your path.

"You have been confused by what has been shown to you from other cultures, but there has been a reason. My father told me when I was sixteen that I would meet you. He said four people representing all the colors would come together and go to a special place to make a prayer. Major changes take place in thirty year periods. In the 1930s was the great depression, in the 1960s was the civil rights movement, and now the 1990s presents all people of the world with the same problem. Our earth is very sick. Its air, water, and land have been poisoned. The time is near for four of us to make a special prayer for the earth. Go and make yourself ready. In your dreams you were the white stick. Maybe you will be one. Make yourself ready. These things my father has shown me in the past and has shown me again this week."

We each had tears, hugged one another, and spoke of being brothers. I thanked Rita and Gary for opening their home to me. They said the sweat lodge is not owned by them and is always open. I told them to let me know if they ever needed any help. We felt like family and with hugs to everyone, I said I would see them soon.

Preparation for a Great Prayer

On the way home the next day, I thought about Gary's words. It was a miracle that the dream of his father had connected with my dream, each illuminating and giving deeper meaning to the other. I knew I was connected to the spirit of Jesus. I now knew more clearly that I was being introduced to other spiritual traditions in order to know them from a level that would enable me to participate in them. In this way perhaps my life was a preparation for some day helping make a great prayer. I also knew these spiritual traditions were teaching me ways of spiritual practice forgotten by the Christian church since the time of Jesus. I was fully appreciative of all my spiritual relatives.

In the world of spirit, there are no ruling powers granted to human beings. Social hierarchies and textual interpretations are the inventions and devices of social institutions. They serve to maintain the social institution that created them and have no necessary connection to spirituality. The old ways, which have not been lost to indigenous people from around the world have all but been extinguished by the Christian churches, Catholic and Protestant. Followers of Jesus need to learn again how to learn from sacred places in the wild, to sweat with the breath of God's sacred stones, to fast and cry for visions, and to live for one's brothers, sisters, and all living creatures of our creator rather than live for oneself. These old ways can be taught to us from other spiritual cultures. We must learn to respect and learn from one another's visions and prayers. The coming together of the four colors of people to make a prayer is also a metaphor for how we must learn to learn from one another.

The North, the time of winter and associated with the color white for cleansing snow, is a spiritual place for preparation and purification (see Ed McGaa, *Mother Earth Spirituality*, San Francisco: Harper, 1990). We make ourselves worthy through rites of purification such as praying in a sweat lodge and, more importantly, through creating and giving work, gifts, and service to others. The emphasis of the path that Jesus walked was serving others. Although this is often obscured in the talk that takes place in expensive cathedrals and churches, it is the main characteristic of the life of Jesus.

The East, the time of spring and associated with the color red for the rising sun, is a place for receiving wisdom, often through the truths voiced by tears and laughter. We seek wisdom through visions, and the practice of Native Americans emphasizes the prayer fast where one cries for a vision empowering one to lead and serve all related beings.

The South, the time of summer and associated with the color yellow for the day sun, is a spiritual place for activating, receiving, moving, and transforming life energy. Many Asian spiritual disciplines have focused on the activation of this energy, whether in the practice of Kundalini yoga or the direct activation and handling of this energy in the Japanese tradition of Seiki-Jutsu. In many cultures sacred music, song, dance, and drumming have been used to arouse and awaken this energy.

The West, the time of fall and associated with the color black for the evening, is the home of the spirits. African spirituality, with its emphasis on direct communication with spirits, typically requires experiencing a half-death or death-of-self that allows for such communion. This communion, known to Native Americans through yuwipi and shaking wigwam ceremonies and to Christians through Holy Spirit baptisms and manifestations, is most directly seen in the practices of African cultures where a person is given to being possessed by the spirits.

All spiritual traditions embody each of these four spiritual directions, although it may be argued that each has developed a particular direction more than the others. Followers of Jesus can therefore learn wisdom from Native Americans, learn about activating energy from the Orient, and learn about communication with the spirits from Africa. All of these traditions, in turn, can learn about sacrifice and service to others from Christians exemplified by Mother Teresa and Martin Luther King, among others.

Some Indian legends prophesize that Jesus will return as a red man. There is truth in this metaphor. Christians may have to learn wisdom from their red brothers and sisters in order to fully meet Jesus again. Other legends from both the Southwest Indians and the Himalayan Tibetans predict a time when East and West will meet. Hopi elders have already met with the Dali Lama and exchanged wisdom. The time has come for us to appreciate, value, and honor our differences. In this way we may learn to make prayers together.

Christ Eagle

In the Spring of 1992, as the time for me to go out and fast drew near, I began to think about what form I should do it in. Although my Ojibway friend Sam was ready to assist me in the Native American tradition, I began pondering over how my most powerful vision had taken place in a chapel when I was a young man. Since that time, I had not tried fasting and praying in a Christian context. The very next day I found out about a hermitage run by two Catholic Sisters in a woods.

I also came across a book by Zora Neal Hurston entitled, *The Sanctified Church*, (Berkeley: Turtle Island, 1983). She notes that the African American church in its early days was very committed to the individual seeking a vision. Visions were sought typically by fasting and praying for three days in a swamp or isolated cemetery. She interviewed several people who were initially unwilling to believe the visions they received and so asked God for proof. In one case, the Lord shot a star across the heavens from left to right when a man asked him to do it. Still not satisfied, he asked for the sun to shout and it shouted. A woman challenged God to move a tree and it moved over ten feet. Another woman asked for a windstorm and it came.

In a testimony by Rev. Jessie Jefferson (Hurston, pp. 89-90), he prayed and fasted in a graveyard. He received a vision where God laid him on a table, split him open, and two men with knives operated on him. When they were through, they touched his wound and healed him. He then got up and saw three bright lights on the table. He was told to reach and grab the brightest one, which they said was his guiding star. He then found he had five white balls in each hand and was told, "Them is the ten tablets I give you." He put the balls inside his breast. Following further instruction, he began shouting and then lay in a swamp through the night.

In consideration of my previous dreams and visions, I realized that many of my most powerful ones had involved direct encounters with Jesus. Furthermore, a place for praying and fasting in a Christian context was nearby and I had discovered that a prayer fast in the wild was a form of spiritual practice for the early day African American church as well as in the earliest days of Christianity.

There were still questions as to my relations with other spiritual traditions. If I was to walk in the path of Jesus, why did I have visions of Native American sacred ways? Why was the dog skull, the way of Sioux healing, revealed to me? Why did I see the holy pipe in my dreams? Why had an elder Indian visited me in a vision and given instruction? Why was I able to become one with the spirit of animals? Also, why was I connecting to African dances, sounds, and body movements? Why was my form of vibratory bodywork found in Africa? Why did I sometimes make Asian sounds and spontaneously assume yogic postures? Why was all of this coming from all directions?

I decided again that it was too much to figure out. I made a prayer the week before I was to fast. I asked for clear direction as to whether I should seek a Christian or Native American context for this practice. I assumed in faith that an answer would come.

I called the wilderness retreat area (mentioned above) supervised by two sisters of the St. Joseph order. They explained that they have 120 acres of woods in a Minnesota state forest with three "hermitages" where one may sit in private silence. Unfortunately, there was no space available when I needed it. They said to call back in a few days to check on any cancellations. I decided to let the availability of a hermitage determine where I would go. If there was a cancellation, which they said was highly unlikely, I would go there. Otherwise, I would head off to the Ojibway reservation.

On the morning when I had to make a decision, a cancellation came through for a hermitage. That was a clear sign. I made arrangements to pray and fast in the state forest. When I arrived at the northern woods area with the hermitages, I was greeted by Chris and Jeanne. These women had been called to find this place in the woods to serve the spiritual journeys of those who came. They respected all sacred paths and supported the uniqueness of every individual's walk.

I immediately sat down with them and we shared stories. It felt comforting and centering to be in their presence. There are very few places one can find where wilderness is set aside for spiritual practice. This, in my opinion, is a service as important as any major university with its libraries, laboratories, and classrooms. The teaching that takes place in the wilderness is essential to our survival as a people and planet.

In my experience in the woods, I was led time and time again to circular configurations — circles of trees, circles of stones, and circles of moss. I would stand in the center of these spaces and pray with all my heart. Once I was told to pray over again immediately after I had prayed all I thought I had to pray. I prayed again and new words with deeper meaning and an increased intensity came forth. *Again*, I was told to pray *again*. *Again*, the prayer became deeper. I felt as if I was being given further instruction in how to pray.

While walking through the woods, I thought I heard a voice and discovered that it was the sound of dry leaves on a maple tree being blown in the wind. I immediately thought that if all things were related, then the movement of the wind, the sound of the leaves, and the thoughts of human minds must be connected. I felt it was possible to communicate with this tree. Placing my head into the limbs of the tree, I closed my eyes and listened.

I immediately had a vision of Jesus on the cross. He opened his white robe, the same robe He had once opened in another vision to show all the animals and living creatures. This time the open robe appeared as wings. His face began to transform into that of an eagle. I wasn't sure if He was an eagle or an ancient thunderbird since the design of the wings looked more like early drawings of the thunderbeings. The cross began to spin counter clockwise and Jesus lifted off the earth and flew through the air. Sometimes I could see His face with a white, superimposed, spirit-like image of an eagle and at other times I saw the eagle's face superimposed upon by the white, spirit-like face of Jesus. He was flying through fire. Fire was everywhere and it was dark. Once the face of this flying bird and cross appeared as my face. The flying continued until the spirit flew into a stream of beautiful water and became a fish.

I had been stunned by the image of Jesus as an eagle or thunderbeing. The integration of a Native American image with a Christian image both amazed me and made me laugh at how strange it would sound to conventional, Christian ears, to say that Jesus is an eagle!

I gave an offering to the tree and then my hand grabbed it and my body began shaking with the tree. The tree moved very wildly back and forth. I then saw a circle of trees and I went into the center, grabbing a tree with each hand. The shaking continued and the trees and I all moved together with intense bursts of energy and movement.

As I walked deeper into the woods, a startling movement took place at the corner of my vision. I didn't see it directly, but it appeared as a large white bird the size of a man or deer flying at mid-height of the trees. Immediately I moved toward where I had seen this and found fourteen white feathers with black stripes at the base of a tree.

I then went to a pool of water nearby and looked down at a beautiful piece of green moss. When I touched it, I realized it was on the top of a buried stone. I was told to dig for this stone. It took all of my energy and effort to dig for it. What appeared to be a small stone turned into a fifty pound boulder. I struggled to pull it out of the mud and water. And then I was shown two other stones to retrieve from the ground in the same manner. One was red, the other black, and both were, again, large stones. I discovered a large white stone but was told to leave it. These stones by the pool of water were arranged in a circle.

I knew I was supposed to carry them out of the wetlands and forest, but I didn't know how I could physically do this. I typically refrain from lifting anything heavy. How could three heavy stones be carried three miles? I prayed that I be given strength to do this if it were the right thing to do.

I proceeded to get my body to vibrate and then reached and lifted a stone to my shoulder. When I carried it as far as my strength would endure, I dropped it and returned to get another stone. And then the same routine for the third stone. Bit by bit I moved each stone this way.

My heart was pounding, I was totally wet with perspiration and felt on the edge of passing out from exhaustion. I had been on a fast for days and there was little energy in my muscles. When I was completely exhausted, I would lie on the ground with my head resting on the largest stone. In this state of complete collapse and surrender, the vision of the flying cross and eagle continued.

I was shown how these stones would be the center piece of my tepee, the tepee of three sticks I had seen in other dreams. I was also shown a dance around a fire within a circle of stones. The dancers moved counterclockwise. This surprised me because I assumed Native American dances followed the clockwise direction of the seasons. I then remembered that this often was the pattern of the Kalahari people's dance.

Step by step, stone by stone, collapsing along the way, and keeping the vision alive took what seemed most of the day. It didn't hit me till later that the stones had provided a different kind of sweat. They had worn me down, made me pray for my life, drenched me in sweat, exhaustion, and surrender. Carrying the stones had brought on vision. I was humbled by the power of these grandfathers.

When the stones were finally brought in, I was told immediately, without any rest, to go and find those three sticks I had been shown in earlier dreams. I went through the woods looking everywhere and couldn't find them. When I returned to my base, I found the three sticks.

Weeks later I discovered that the eagle was an early figure for depicting Christ and that the eagle was placed on Christian lamps in the fourth century in Carthage (see Louis Charbonneau-Lassay, *The Bestiary of Christ*, New York: Arkana Books, 1992). On these lamps were drawn two stars or lights, one on each side of the eagle's head.

I also learned that ancient peoples saw the eagle as a carrier of light and fire and that the symbolism of Christ as fire and light was part of ancient Christian understanding. Most astonishingly, I discovered old tales of the Orient where the eagle was depicted as getting so close to the fire of the divine star that its feathers became charred. When it returned to earth, it plunged into spring water and became regenerated.

Light That Flickers in the East

When I returned home, I told Marian about my experiences and shared with her that during one of my prayers I had heard her voice. It was not a voice inside me; I literally heard her say something near me. I even turned to see if she was there. She said she had been praying at that time and had spoken the words I heard. We were both moved by the power of prayer.

I also received a call from Wendel, a close colleague in Louisiana. I was consulting on a case of his involving a couple there. Following an intervention we had given them, an unusual event took place. They were driving down the highway when they saw a great horned owl standing in the middle of the road. They stopped, assuming the owl was injured. The man went up to the owl and it stared directly into his eyes. The man offered tobacco and took its middle feather. The owl then flew off.

The man went on to say that he had met a relative of Black Elk when he was a child. Furthermore, many years before, he had noticed an advertisement in a paper that he couldn't believe. A museum curator was selling Black Elk's holy rattle. He purchased it and now had it in his home. Once he shook it and a violent storm immediately took place, scaring him out of ever thinking of using it again. I knew this story would bring a special meaning to my journey, although I couldn't understand how at the moment.

On the same day that I heard the Black Elk story, my Ojibway friend made arrangements to take me north near the Canadian border to meet another Ojibway medicine man. He was a gifted man described as one who "sees things." I prepared to visit him and ask his help with respect to what I was to do with what I was being shown in my dreams.

In driving north to see this man, I reflected on how I believed love and humility to be closely related. Love is sometimes confused with the desire to possess and consume. When one feels obsessed with desire for anything, whether it be a precious stone, money, a person, success, or experience, love is absent. Lust, desire, and mad devotion are not related to humility. They are more connected with pride, ownership, conquest, and consumption. Love, in its purest form, requires the absence of self and the presence of a reverance for all relationships. This love serves rather than consumes, sacrifices rather than demands, and is humble rather than proud.

A spiritual teacher was once asked, "How do you know if your dreams and visions are from God?" The response was, "If you are made more humble after the dream, it was from God." The meaning of one's spiritual life is found in the action it breeds. Having dreams of ecstasy does not make one spiritual. If it fills one with pride and blindness to the needs of others, it's a curse. If it makes one less aware of one's self and more aware of others, it's from God. Enlightenment is not a light that enables you to discover, realize, encounter, develop, or actualize your ordinary self. It is turning the spotlight off of one's self. In this new darkness, the lights of others may be seen. In this way we see with the spiritual eyes of God. We are able to serve others employing different vision, different hearing, different touch, different understanding, and different love.

Wisdom does not come from any particular source. Wisdom is the result of how we transform and utilize all sources. Since all living things are related, any part is capable of speaking (or listening) for the whole. The sound of the whole is healing wisdom and evokes all of life.

Talking, listening, and making offerings to trees, plants, wingeds, four-leggeds, insects, stones, and so forth, is not about giving privilege or special status to other living organisms. It is a way of enacting our relationship with all of creation. What we would want done to us, we do to others.

What is given by other living things is nothing without someone who makes something out of it. We are not passive receivers or receptors of truth; we must create it. Creation is action, acting upon what others may not see, hear, feel, or understand and transforming it into the seen, heard, felt, and understood. Medicine is something made out of nothing by the relationship of the giver and receiver. Both are healed by the enactment of their faith in this joint dance of co-creation.

When I met the Ojibway medicine man near the Canadian border, I discovered he was the leader of the area's Midéwiwin (medicine) lodge. Because of his request for strict confidentiality, I will not mention his name or the exact location where he lives. When we met, he immediately said the spirits had discussed me the night before. They told him I was originally from a very, very, distant place in the galaxy. There was a star and a spirit even higher than where the UFO's come from. This place was called "the third sky."

The spirit told him I was good and that everything happening to me was good. Many people who had been granted spiritual vision and gifts were unable to bear it and they turned to various addictions and exploitations to escape, whether with drugs, gambling, or otherwise. He said none of this was in me and that good was present. Furthermore, I should never give up faith in being good.

Long ago, he said, a small bow and arrow had been placed inside my hands. I was called to heal with my hands. People of all colors would start coming to me with all kinds of disease, including blindness and cancer. My responsibility was to heal them with my hands. He said I really didn't need any spiritual tools or devices, that the power in my hands was enough.

All of this he told without hearing my whole story. He had correctly identified my hands as the locus of my healing work. When I told him my story, he gave me more details about my principal spirit guide. We eventually went to his special room, and he performed a ceremony to bring forth his spirit guides. I was able to see these spirits in my mind's eye and correctly answer questions as to what I saw. The encounter was extremely powerful, particularly when a spirit bear opened my chest with his claws and created a hole in the center of my body.

The spirits told me a story that I am not permitted to tell. I was also informed that what I had seen in the woods the week prior to my visit was a white eagle. I was then given directions to make and find some things.

I discovered that the head of another Midéwiwin lodge had been directly approached by Jesus who told him how to heal. The man had Jesus in his heart along with other spirit guides. I was humbled by how Midéwiwin members supported the unique spiritual development and practice of each medicine person. There were no rigid templates specifying how healing should be done by everyone. Each person was very different and obedient to what the spirits had told and shown them.

The next morning while it was still dark, I was told to look outside and something would be shown. I looked due east and saw a flash of light that looked like a star near the horizon. When I looked again, the light flashed one more time. Then it disappeared. Later that day I told the medicine man that the Cheyenne medicine man, William Tallbull, had told me the spirits would soon give me a name. I was aware that a person could have several, perhaps many, spirit names. At one time the name, "Little Singing Thunder" had come to me. The Ojibway man immediately said, "I heard the spirits say a name this morning. It was, 'Light that Flickers in the East.'" I was reminded of the old Carthage lamps with a flickering light on each side of an eagle's head depicting Christ. I knew my shamanic journey was associated with the light flickering in the east and that this light was the holy light connected with Christ. I would find, however, that it wouldn't be until I returned to Africa again that I formally would be given my spirit name.

The Gnostic Gospels
and the Dance of Christ

To understand that there is a connection between Jesus and the spiritual practices of the Bushmen and Native American Indians requires a little historical investigation. In 1945, an Egyptian peasant dug up a red jar, almost a meter high, and broke it thinking it might contain gold. What was discovered was a collection of thirteen papyrus books that proved to be what are now commonly referred to as "the Gnostic Gospels." The first line of one of these texts reads, "These are the secret words which the living Jesus spoke, and which the twin, Judas Thomas, wrote down" (Elaine Pagels, *The Gnostic Gospels*, New York: Vintage, 1979, p.xv). What Muhammad Ali, the peasant, discovered at Nag Hammadi, were Coptic translations made about 1,500 years ago of still more ancient manuscripts originally written in Greek. The original manuscripts are argued to be as early as, or even earlier than, the biblical books of *Mark, Matthew, Luke,* and *John.* Fragments of some these books had survived in the commentaries of Christian writers who opposed their message, but, for the most part, these writings had been suppressed. The suppression of these books by the official church was a necessity given the fact their message was not only mystical, but clearly anti-institutional. Their basic teaching is to develop a form of inner knowing or "gnosis." Jesus is seen not as coming to save us from sin, but as a spiritual guide. When the disciple is enlightened, Jesus, the teacher, becomes one with the student: the two become equal and identical. This identity is expressed as becoming the "twin of Jesus."

The resurrected Christ appears to people in spiritual visions. Mary Magdalene, the first to see the risen Christ, asked Jesus how one sees Him and He answered that He is seen through the spiritually aware mind. Gnostics claim that whoever "sees the Lord" through spiritual vision "can claim that his or her own authority equals, or surpasses, that of the twelve." (Pagels, pp. 13-14). Christ is alive in the spiritual visions revealed to spiritual seekers.

In *II Corinthians 12: 1-10*, Paul writes of being "caught up to the third heaven — whether in the body or out of the body I do not know." Here "he heard things that cannot be told, which man may not utter." The Midéwiwin man told me my spirit and spirit guide come from the "third sky." In the commentary to *The New Oxford Annotated Bible*, (p.1407) "the third heaven" is noted as referring to "the highest bliss." It also suggests that the scriptural phrase, "things that cannot be told", means "Paul cannot tell these things because they are too sacred."

Paul goes on to say, "And to keep me from being too elated by the abundance of revelations, a thorn was given me in the flesh, a messenger of Satan, to harass me, to keep me from being too elated." It seems that all who receive great spiritual gifts must also carry a burden, thorn, pain, or suffering. Otherwise, one would too easily lose one's humility, a requisite for being filled with spirit. Only when we are weak, nothing, and humble can spirit come to us. When Paul asked the Lord to remove this thorn, the Lord said, "for my power is made perfect in weakness." Realizing that he had to be weak to receive the Lord, he proclaimed, "I will all the more gladly boast of my weaknesses, that the power of Christ may rest upon me."

In *The Acts of John,* one of the most famous gnostic texts, Jesus is described as joined with His disciples in Gethsemane just prior to being arrested. What follows from this text sent a chill through my whole body when I first read it because it took aim at the very center of the connections I was finding between different cultural spiritual practices around the earth. The gnostic book states:

> He assembled us all, and said, 'before I am delivered to them, let us sing a hymn to the Father, and so go to meet what lies before (us).' So He told us to form a circle, holding one another's hands, and Himself stood in the middle.

He then began a mystical chant, which reads, in part:

> "I will pipe,
> Dance, all of you. — amen.
> I will mourn,
> Beat you all your breasts. — amen.
> The one Ogdoad
> Sings praises with us. — amen.
> The twelfth number
> dances on high. — amen.
> "To the Universe belongs the dancer." — amen."

> "He who does not dance does not know what
> happens." — amen" . . .
> "Now if you follow my dance, see yourself in
> Me who am speaking
> and when you have seen what I do,
> keep silence about my mysteries.
> You who dance, consider what I do, for yours is
> This passion of Man which I am to suffer.
> For you could by no means have understood what
> you suffer unless to you as Logos I
> had been sent by the Father . . . Learn how to
> suffer and you shall be able not to suffer. . .

After the Lord had danced with us, my beloved, he went out (to suffer). And we were like men amazed or fast asleep, and we fled this way and that. And so I saw him suffer, and did not wait by his suffering, but fled to the Mount of Olives and wept. And when he was hung (upon the Cross) on Friday, at the sixth hour of the day there came a darkness over the whole earth."

At that very instant, John who was sitting in a cave in Gethsemane saw a vision of Jesus who said: "John for the people below . . . I am being crucified and pierced with lances. . . But to you I am speaking, and listen to what I speak." Then the vision showed John a "cross of light" and said, "I have suffered none of the things which they will say of me; even that suffering which I showed to you and to the rest in my dance, I will that it be called a mystery.

Approximately one hundred years ago, an unusual report was transmitted through the United States War Department (see James Mooney, *The Ghost Dance Religion and Wounded Knee*, New York: Dover, 1973). The report stated that Jesus Christ appeared at Walkers Lake, Esmeralda County, Nevada. Indians and white people were dancing together at this place. The government report claims that Jesus gathered with a large number of Indians and taught them a dance. He sang while they danced. As he sang, he shook and trembled all over, sometimes violently. He then lay down and appeared dead. After a while, he awakened and said He had visited His Father. The Holy Father had said it was time to renew the earth. If the people were good, He would send healers to heal by mere touch. He said that the Indians and whites were to be one people and that He was available to everyone in their spiritual vision.

This dance, which became known as the "Ghost Dance," was the same dance of Jesus in the Gnostic Gospels. I believe it may also be the healing dance of the Kalahari Bushmen.

The appearance of another ring dance leading to shaking and healing is found among the so-called "Indian Shakers" (see H. G. Barrett, *Indian Shakers*, Carbondale, Ill.: Southern Illinois Press, 1957). In 1881, a forty-year-old Indian from Puget Sound named John Slocum fell sick and supposedly died. While mourners waited for his coffin to arrive, he was resurrected and spoke of being confronted by a shining light. About a year later, he fell ill again. This time his wife, Mary Slocum, had a possession experience and went to her husband's prostrate body praying, sobbing, trembling, dancing, and wildly shaking. John Slocum recovered and Mary's shaking was held as divine in origin.

Her shaking began when she felt something hot flow over her body, making her tremble. She took no credit for her healing and her husband announced that it was available to everyone. Most interestingly, this shaking could be transmitted from one person to another. The shake, as a medicine, had curative and restorative properties that brought about mental and physical relief. Indian shakers sometimes had visions when under the influence of shaking, enabling them to see the future, foretell deaths, and find lost objects. Songs were often given by the spirits to those being shaken.

In their rituals, Indian shakers typically revolved in circular processions going counterclockwise. Much like the Kalahari dancers, the shakers weave in and out of the circle until the shaking comes upon someone. At this point the healer's fluttering hands are placed over another person's body, all the while singing and chanting.

In these historical stories, a great mystery is revealed. In the dance of Christ, the Bushmen's healing dance, and the Native American Indian Ghost Dance, people are found shaking, healing with their hands, and having great visions. My shamanic journey was uncovering a pattern connecting the spiritual practices of these diverse traditions.

A Spiritual Medicine Wheel

As I began to discover how shaking was related to spiritual practices in different traditions, I was shown in a vision how to arrange a red stick, yellow stick, and black stick in the directions of east, south, and west, respectively. In the center of this arrangement were the stones I received in the woods. They came together in such a way that my head fit perfectly in the center space of them. The red stone was placed in the east. It had what appeared as the claw print of an eagle on it. The yellow stone, for the south, appeared as the mid-body section of a four-legged. The stone for the west, the largest of all the stones, was red with black specks except for the west side, which had a crack and was colored black. It appeared as a large animal skull. The northern stone was a smaller white one in the shape of a dog's skull.

A spirit animal was associated with each direction: the eagle for the east, wolf for the south, bear for the west, and buffalo for the center. In the middle of the stones, I was to place some sacred objects. And directly over the stones I was to hang the eagle feather, originally given to me by the Ojibway medicine man. This spiritual tool was to be used in the following manner: I would lay my head on the middle of the four stones and seek vision. A time was coming when its specific purpose would be made more clear. My presence as the stick of the north overlapped with the dream of Gary Holy Bull's father. In that dream, four different spiritual traditions would come together and make a prayer for the earth. This dream fit my own vision of the sticks, representing the way I practiced and connected with each of these spiritual ways. Yellowtail, the great Crow medicine man, once spoke these words (in Michael O. Fitzgerald, *Yellowtail: Crow Medicine Man and Sun Dance Chief;* Norman: University of Oklahoma Press, 1991, pp. 198-199):

"As we know, this earth is round like a wagon wheel. In a wagon wheel, all the spokes are set into the center. The circle of the wheel is round, and all spokes

come from the center, and the center is You, Acbadadea, the Maker of All Things Above. Each spoke can be considered as a different religion of the world, which has to be given by you to different people and different races. All of the people of the world are on the rim of the wheel . . . The different paths have been given to us, but they all lead to the same place. We all pray to the same God, to you. There are different places on the wheel, so each way may look strange to someone following a different path. It is easy for people to say that their way is the best if they know all about their faith and it is good for them. But they should refrain from saying bad things about other ways that they don't know about. There should be no hard feelings about someone else if he is following a way that leads to You. Help us to see this wisdom."

My visions and spiritual practice were clearly becoming that of a spiritual medicine wheel. I was understanding the practices and resources of different spiritual traditions as distinct and joined, unique and related, partial and whole. My spiritual journey had begun with seeing a great light and being shaken to the core. As I moved through different spiritual traditions, I continued seeing light and being shaken. My next journey to Africa was soon to come, followed by trips to South America in August, 1992, and Japan in October, 1992. Each was a movement around the spiritual wheel.

A Flood of Vision

A week following my visit to the leader of the Midéwiwin lodge in April, 1992, I had several very vivid dreams and visions I did not understand. In one, the name "Mahari" was mentioned to me as belonging to someone who would later give me something important. In another vision, I clearly saw a smooth, cave-like stone structure with two doors. Inside this chamber was a sword standing in the ground in front of what

I assumed was a tomb. The handle of the sword contained an emerald and on the floor in front of the sword was a large figure "X" in white light.

That very morning, out of thin air, two books of mine disappeared. One book was on Ojibway dreaming and the other on the Sanctified (African American) Church. The books had never been removed from my office and yet they vanished. My assumption was that there was significance in the fact that these two particular books had disappeared. My path was discovering a convergence between the two traditions these books represented.

At the moment of this insight, I called the Midéwiwin leader and he immediately communicated he had been expecting to hear from me. The spirits had shown him more specific details about a book that should be written on spiritual truth, much of it being about Jesus. He said that when I returned from Africa, he and I would take a trip into the interior of Ontario, one day by car and two days by canoe, to meet a very holy man who shakes the wigwam. He said, "There we would directly talk with Jesus and find what He wants to be said."

How could it be that, wherever I went, whether to the heart of the Kalahari in Africa or the waterways of Ontario, Jesus was the center of my encounter with these variant cultural healing traditions? Prior to traveling to Africa, I had found that the Kalahari healing dance was similar to the dance Jesus gave to his disciples the night before his crucifixion. In my encounter with the Midéwiwin, I was being led to a man who could bring forth the presence of Jesus.

At times I would laugh at the thought of how absurd all of this must sound to spiritually uninitiated ears. At other times, I was humbled by the way these great spiritual doors were being opened to move me forward on this journey. I knew this was my life and whether I was labeled as psychotic as a hoot owl was irrelevant. I'd rather be mad with a good heart, doing the least harm, than be sane in the way contemporary culture defined sanity, reason, good, and spiritual. I knew that those propagandized definitions often led to harm and were toxically dissociated from the great spiritual truths.

A change came over me in the weeks preceding my trip to Africa. I began praying even more sincerely than I had thought possible. I asked to be rid of my selfishness, pride, and sense of importance. My prayers turned away from being centrally focused on my concerns and were given to help, strengthen, and support other people.

After a particular prayer meeting, the head deacons came to me and asked if I would serve as a deacon in the church. I was immediately unable to speak and filled with a sense of being unworthy. How could the only white man in the church be accepted for such a responsibility? I told them

I only wanted to serve and would be willing to do any work such as being the janitor. They said they wanted me to participate in the spiritual leadership of the church. I was so nervous I shook inside and don't even remember what I said other than I would pray hard about it. The next evening these two deacons and I held hands in the church basement and prayed for the Lord to lead me to how I was to serve in the church.

The Seven Skies

In the spring of 1992, about a week after building the spiritual tepee, I felt called to use it. Within the tepee, as I mentioned above, was an inner circle formed from the stones I had brought out of the North woods. This space was for resting my head. To the south, west, and east were three differently colored sticks, and, hanging down the center of this tepee was a string with an eagle feather attached at the bottom. The feather was directly above my head when I would lay my head on the stones. In the center of the stones was a bed of tobacco, covered with the partridge feathers that the white eagle had led me to with a leaf from the tree that gave me the vision of Christ as an eagle.

I had known that a time would come when I would learn what this spiritual instrument was intended to be used for. On the night when I learned to use it, a family member had been admitted to the hospital for exploratory surgery for an undetermined infection. A team of specialists had been unable to diagnose what was going on. I prayed for him, and, following those prayers, I felt called to enter the spiritual tepee and lay my head on the stones and wait for direction.

When my head was resting on the stones, I immediately saw the eagle feather hovering over me. I remembered the time on the cliff when my heart merged with the eagle and taught me to be one with its spirit. With this remembrance of my heart, I saw the string as a ladder to the heavens and viewed the tripod as reaching way beyond the clouds. With the eagle in my heart, I was carried high into the sky as far as the eagle can fly. There I came through a cloud and saw a white angel holding a brass trumpet. I thought this must be Gabriel. He immediately began playing the horn and the most beautiful full sound of a trumpet came forth. A full orchestra joined him in the background, and I listened to him play what to me is the most moving hymn ever written, "Precious Lord."

The music of the heavens lifted me to a new height. It provided wings that took me higher than the highest place the eagles can go. I was lifted through another cloud and saw a rainbow with seven white angels sitting on it. Each angel was holding an open book, which I presumed was the Bible. As I absorbed this sight, I was filled with the realization that we are unable to receive holy words unless our hearts are lifted this high. With that insight, I was immediately filled with an understanding that lifted me higher than the rainbow. Over the rainbow sat the Buddha with crossed legs in meditative fashion, with what looked like a large black "V" over-lapping his solar plexus. As I focused on this image, I saw this as the location for focusing all one's mind on one point of singular vision. At that very moment the Buddha slowly fell on his back like a lever or door being opened and the V on his midsection turned into an array of brilliant white light rays. Following these rays of light upward led me to another height, the place of Jesus.

I asked Jesus to heal this man. Jesus placed his hands in my hands and the next scene I saw was a laser-like light opening the man's head and filling it with light. His spine was then opened by the light and seven stars entered his midsection. These stars joined as a circle and moved as a ring dance through his insides. Jesus then said, "He has received all he needs." The doctors subsequently discovered the infection and he became well again.

I quickly went to my Bible and looked up scripture associated with Gabriel. The first reference I found was Daniel 8:16, "And I heard a man's voice between the banks of Ulai, which called, and said, Gabriel, make this man understand the vision." I knew what this meant. Gabriel, with his music, could fill a man's heart in such a way that understanding was possible.

I then turned to look for the meaning of seven angels and seven stars and found Revelation 1:20,"The mystery of the seven stars which thou sawest in my right hand. . . The seven stars are the angels of the seven churches. . . " In the commentary of *The New Oxford Annotated Bible* (p.1443) is the notion that "seven suggests the idea of completeness and totality" and that "the seven spirits who are before his throne" referred to in Revelation 1:4 refer to "either angelic beings or, more likely, a symbolic reference to the manifold energies of the Spirit of God."

The meaning of my three previous dreams was clear to me. The spiritual tepee was a ladder to the heavens. The ascension itself involved seven levels: (1) man with his heart; (2) flying with the eagle spirit; (3) to the music of Gabriel; (4) enabling the rainbow with its understanding of holy words to be seen; (5) Here, the singular focus of Buddha; (6) takes one to the light of Christ; and (7) God, the creator above Christ. I knew this ladder was a way to reach the holy light. Following prayer that opens my heart, I could rest my head on the stones and fly with the eagle to the clouds where celestial music is heard. From there, one could be lifted to the understanding that emanates from the seven spirits of the rainbow. In turn, that understanding lifts one to the place of Buddha's focus and centeredness, a door opening one to the light of Jesus. Through Jesus, spiritual work and healing could be done.

The Great Prophecies

Soon after this vision, I was introduced to the great prophecy of the Hopis. They say we are entering the "final days" and that an "Elder White Brother" will come to them. He will be recognized by his bringing a missing piece of a stone tablet and by his having had a vision of what the sacred tablets mean (see Rudolf Kaiser, *The Voice of the Great Spirit*, Boston: Shambhala, 1991.) Thomas Banyacya of Oraibi, Arizona (in Kaiser, pp.39-45), stated in a letter that the prophecies declare the human race has passed through three stages of life. At the end of each stage is a purification by the Great Spirit, the last one being a great flood. At that time, a few faithful ones, including the Hopi, were spared their lives by promising to the Great Spirit they would live a "poor, humble, and simple life."

The letter told of a set of sacred stone tablets that were given to two brothers with instructions where to go. The older brother headed out to the East and was told he would return when a great white star appeared in the sky. Over many years the older brother's skin would change to white and he would have the ability to write things down and be the only one able to read the Sacred Stone Tablets. The letter ends as follows (pp. 44-45 in Kaiser):

> Now the evil white man is about to take away our last remaining homeland. We are still being denied many things including the right to be Hopis and to make our livelihood in accordance with our religious teachings. . .
> We now stand at the crossroad whether to lead ourselves into everlasting life or (into) total destruction. The Hopi still holds the Sacred Stone Tablets and is now waiting for the coming of his true white brother.

The various cultures and spiritual traditions of the world await the turning of white people away from materialism and greed and the movement toward stewardship and service. The final vision of the Teton Sioux Chief, Crazy Horse, rejoices in this change and the reuniting of people it will bring (Vinson Brown, *Voices of Earth and Sky*, Harrisburg, Penn., 1974, p.166):

> He saw his people being driven into spiritual darkness and poverty while white people prospered in a material way all around them, but even in the darkest times he saw that the eyes of a few of his people kept the light of dawn and the wisdom of the earth, which they passed on to some of their grandchildren. He saw the coming of automobiles and airplanes and twice he saw the great darkness and heard the screams and explosions when millions died in two great world wars.
> But after the second great war passed, he saw a time come when his people began to awaken, not all at once, but a few here and there and then more and more, he saw that they were dancing in the beautiful light of the Spirit World under the Sacred Tree even while still on earth. Then he was amazed to see that dancing under that tree were representatives of all races who had become brothers, and he realized that the world would

be made new again and in peace and harmony not just by his people, but by members of all the races of mankind.

Diane Meili, great-granddaughter of well-known Cree elder, Victoria Callihoo, wrote a beautiful collection of testimonies from Alberta's native elders, entitled, *Those Who Know* (Edmonton: NeWest Pub., 1991). In this book she writes about a spiritual man named Albert Lightning. He spoke of "his visit 'upstairs' to see the Great Spirit" and about "the second coming of Christ." He saw no difference between religions and argued that "the next century will be spiritual or it will not be at all" (p.82). The essence of his message, Meili summarizes, is "when you see the right thing to do, hold on to it firmly and don't look at material conditions or consequences. The Creator has planted seeds of truth in you so you know the right thing to do." Albert also believed, "it's time we stop being secretive about our beliefs and experiences and share them with the world because the world needs it."

When I first heard of Albert Lightning, I felt a special connection I did not understand. It wouldn't be until much later in my journey of initiation that I would learn what this connection meant.

Albert Lightning

Preparation for the Kalahari

Prior to departing for Africa in May, 1992, I made contact with Rick Lightning, the medicine man from Alberta, Canada, whose father, the holy man Albert Lightning, had passed away the previous year. Rick said Albert recently appeared to an elder, telling him his life was much the same on the other side where he continued praying for all his relatives as he had done on earth. Rather than occasionally passing over to visit the spiritual world he now intermittently passed over to visit earth. He said it was very beautiful in the spirit world.

Rick Lightning passed his blessings to the Bushmen of Africa. He reminded me to focus on the purpose of my trip. When I told him about the healing dance, he explained how a particular spiritual dance is sometimes given to a person. Rick mentioned most medicine people are given the stewardship and responsibility of a dance to use and that my vision of the trip's purpose fits this understanding.

As the final days preceding my departure to Africa came, I prayed harder about whether I was supposed to go. Many people, including friends and medicine people, expressed their concern for my safety on this trip. My previous premonitions about dying in Africa came back to haunt me and fear about the trip arose. My mother even flew out to see me the week before my trip, expressing her concern as to whether she would ever see me again. She asked to make my final legal preparations in the event I did not return. During the last church service I attended before leaving, several people in the church spontaneously began talking about how their lives had been previously spared due to canceling a trip or a car ride somewhere, finding out later that a major accident took place on the route they would have traveled.

I honestly did not know whether this was a message for me not to go or whether it was a test for me to walk with faith through the fires of fear. I prayed and believed I must go. I was prepared to die and if this was my destiny, I would accept it. I continued to feel I would die a spiritual death, the death of who I had been and rebirth into a new way of being and understanding.

The day before I left, I received a tape of spiritual songs I had composed, which were sung and recorded by Camelia and La Shanta, African American gospel singers from Chicago. For the first time I could really hear how the songs I had written were meant to be heard. The songs finally had been born. They were moving and fed my spiritual being, helping provide a knowing that it was right to go to Africa. The music healed my worries and filled my heart with great hope. Immediately I went to my minister and played him the tape. With tears in his eyes, he looked into my eyes and we both embraced, knowing these songs had come from the Holy Spirit. Following our celebration of the music, Rev. McAfee said he knew it was right to go to Africa and that I must do so. Furthermore, he fully expected to see me return.

On the plane to South Africa, I sat next to a physician from Johanessburg. As we became acquainted on the seventeen hour flight from New York City, he told me a story about a Bushman. During the filming of the internationally popular film, "The Gods Must Be Crazy," something happened to the star of the film. This man, G/aqo /'hana, was seen one day as impossible to communicate with. He appeared to be in a trance and his whole body was shaking. The physician telling me this story was the doctor called in to treat the man. After administering physical tests, nothing could be found that was wrong. He shook for two straight days and then came out of it. The doctor and staff assumed he was overwhelmed by being plunged into modern civilization and that his two-day experience was some sort of stress response. He had no idea that the man may have been having a spiritual healing experience. The story was a gift to me, making me mindful of the purpose of my trip. I was journeying across the world to encounter others familiar with shaking spirits.

Home Again In Africa

My arrival in Africa felt like a homecoming. I was greeted by my friends, Peter and Ansie, who are like family to me. It was Peter who would be accompanying me into the Kalahari. He had worked throughout the year to make the necessary arrangements for the trip.

Ansie had found the location of a woman healer I mentioned to her. I had read about Mama Mona in a book of interviews with major healers from around the world (Nancy and Esmond Gardner (Eds.), *Five Great Healers Speak Here.* London: Quest, 1982). Mama Mona and her husband had started a Spiritualist church and devoted their entire life to healing. I told Ansie about her and asked if she might inquire as to where she was located. I had no idea where she lived in Africa. Ansie found the woman in Soweto, contacted her, and set up a meeting for us.

In addition, Ansie made arrangements for us to go to Zululand, where a healing center had been established years ago by a German man. It had a hospital with over a hundred beds. No drugs were given there, only the spiritual medicine of prayer. We were going to spend the weekend participating in their healing ceremonies.

Within the first few days in Africa, I met with my friend Stan with whom I had had many powerful spiritual experiences during my first visit to Africa. We went to his house and shared stories about the journeys we had taken since we last met. I told him how I had taken his special room with me. The room in his house filled with sacred objects had become part of my mind, and sometimes when working with someone, it would come to me and the spirits of that room would come forth. In particular, one mask was a door to very powerful forces I would sometimes be led to when healing others.

I showed him the mask and told him it was in me. He said he was once told that when he found that mask, it would be the last mask he would ever have to find. All other things found after it were only complementary pieces to its presence. We then talked about what we acknowledged was confusing to most people. This discussion was on the association of evil or dark with all that is good and light.

I told him how I had seen the Holy Grail as the still point between good and evil. At that center point any transformation is possible. Here anything could be changed into anything. When sitting in the midst of a spiritual experience, it is important to stay in its center point. To indulge in moving toward absorbing its goodness or badness was to lose one's place in the center. In this respect it is as much an error to overindulge in the experience of good and light as it is to dwell too long in the dark.

Stan pulled out a book by the African writer and sangoma, Credo Mutwa, and read the following passage that crisply underscored this insight (Credo Mutwa, *Indaba My Children*, London: 1966, p.460):

> The two "worm-like" creatures you saw inside each soul were Good and Evil. But let me explain this in greater detail. The red "worm" stands for all bad things in a man or a woman — dishonesty, cruelty, pride, low cunning, spiritual and corporal perversity, cowardice, low morality. The royal blue worm stands for all the good in a human being or an animal — loyalty, courage, honesty, love, and charity. These worm-like components help to balance the soul. A combination of good and evil, equally balanced, is essential — for all souls that exist, like all living creatures, must have a perfect balance between life and death. If a man, for instance, should have only good qualities, without any bad qualities for balance, he would have no reason for existing at all. The same with a soul if it has only the blue worm, the soul becomes automatically destroyed.
>
> This is why people who are really good, never live long. The two "worms" are always quarreling and when one hurts the other, the soul is temporarily unbalanced. If it happens to be the red worm that hurts the blue worm, then the man inhabited by the soul becomes evil — he becomes a thief, a murderer, and even worse. The law of our fathers say that we must kill such a man, kill him so that the soul also may be destroyed. If a man becomes very good, the highest example of virtue, then we must pray to the gods to bring this man to an early grave, because although he is good, his body and soul have lost their balance and such a man has forfeited his right to exist in a world in which anything can happen when people are not normal and balanced.

All healers, whether in Africa, North and South America, or Asia, know that spiritual work takes place between the poles of light and dark and that good and evil are always copresent. Even the symbolism of the cross can be understood as the intersection of two opposing pairs of opposites. The point in the center is the place of great stillness and transformation. Here healing takes place through the balancing of all imaginable differences and vibrations.

According to Wolfram (cited in Carl Jung and Von Franz, *The Grail Legend*, Boston: Sigo Press, 1980, p. 150), the Holy Grail was guarded by "those angels who had remained neutral during the strife between God and Satan." Those angels sought a position of balance between evil and good. The point between God and Satan, evil and good, dark and light, or any pair of oppositions is the very locus of transformation where one side crosses into the other.

The temptation of all spiritual walks is to leave this center point and become infatuated with any particular side, good or evil, light or dark. To do so is to inflate one's self and lose the emptiness required to be an instrument for holy healing work. Anyone's inflation of self must be healed by hanging one's self across all four corners. All opposing contrasts then have to be embraced in this crucifixion, where self is sacrificed in order for spiritual birth to reawaken.

The Vision of Understanding

I was awakened in the middle of the third night of my trip in Africa and told to get out of bed and pray hard. Following this prayer, the face of a large eagle came and physically moved me with a bolt of energy. I entered into this eagle and flew with it to Soweto where I encountered the woman healer, Mama Mona. She had just had eye surgery and in this vision I removed my eyes (the eagle's eyes) and placed them in hers.

When I returned I was shown the image of doing healing work between a cross on my right and the mask of evil on my left. In the center was the place of greatest healing energy where I was to remain.

I was then jolted in bed by the appearance of a black snake's head popping out of my belly. I immediately grabbed it and held onto it. My body began wiggling like a snake and I became a snake making the appropriate tongue movements and sounds. I looked straight into the snake's face, whose eyes were bright red, and faced the fear of snakes I'd had all of my life.

I then knew this snake was to live within me so I forced it back into my belly and felt it move inside me. A song was given and I knew that more work would take place. Immediately I realized I had to contact Jesus. I prayed for Him, shouted for Him, and reached for Him. A dark cross appeared and I stretched out on it. I knew it was absolutely necessary to find Him that very moment. He appeared and I opened my hands for Him. With my deepest desire I placed Him into my body, with His heart resting in the area of my own heart. A sense of wholeness and balance took place with Jesus's heart in my heart and the red-eyed black snake in the bottom of my belly.

Many songs came into my heart then, including the spiritual music I had written. In this ecstasy of sound, I lifted my heart very high into the spirit realm. And the voice of the Great Spirit came and spoke to me. It said:

"You will soon be told what you finally need to know. The last piece of understanding you have sought will be given. This will be given to you in the future. This will be given to you now.

"It all began with what you know as Africa. This was the beginning when the world was flat. It was the plate off of which I ate. And then one day the insects broke through the earth. These were the white people and they brought evil and disease to the world. The holes they created in the earth started a filling and moving within the earth and the flat plate of Africa began to turn into a ball and other places were born. The earth as you know it was created in this way.

"The penis of the Great Spirit, which is around your penis and all other men, is the mamba snake. It was placed inside the jaws of the crocodile. This very large penis snake entirely filled the crocodile's insides. The crocodile chewed up your penis as it is doing this very moment and the crocodile is now getting sick and is vomiting. See what it has spit out. It has vomited forth its teeth. You are now to find these crocodile teeth. They are waiting to be worn around your neck.

"Know that the four directions created by the new world came to be with the birth of the four colors of people. Out of the blood from the crocodile's chewing the snake came the red people. Out of the yolk of the crocodile egg came the yellow people. Out of the snake of God's penis came the black people

and out of the insects came the white people. Someday you will eat all these things to bring them together as one.

"And with this knowledge you must now cry, as I, the Great Spirit, once cried when the insects changed my flat plate. Think of your grandfather and your son and let them open your sadness and joy. They will bring the tears to your face. As the tears drop, touch them with your right hand and let the snake tongue of your mouth lick and swallow them into your belly. Know that these same tears made all the great waters of the earth. Know this and heal with this.

"Know that in these great showers of tears, the earth began to become green. The green ones then appeared and the Great Spirit became filled with great joy. The trees enabled the wind to be heard and songs were born. With this joy of sound, the Great Spirit gave earth the son of his sun, the holy light. You know him as Jesus. He is the light, the literal son of the Holy sun, the same one the Egyptians knew.

"Know that it is time for you to jump off the top of the waterfall. Stare at the different light beams. With single mindedness and attention, make them converge as one and jump. Stop at the middle of the water fall. There in the white cloud is Jesus. He will tell you about the fire in your hands. And Jesus said, 'Look into your right hand and see. Both of your hands are on fire. Your left hand is on your belly and it is very hot. It holds the heat of the snake. Your right hand is connected to me. Look into it. See what is shown.'"

Then I saw a tunnel with a beam of light. I knew I was being taken to the other side, the place of our ancestors. At first it was very dark and a sense of things I did not want to pay attention to organized my movement. And then there was an opening up ahead on the left side where light was coming out. I was told not to go in, because I might not ever come back. This was because my ancestors wouldn't want me to leave. I felt I wanted to go in anyway and started to move toward it, but I stopped. A mirror was placed in the corner enabling me to encounter my ancestors. My grandfather was there. I could hear him like I heard him as a child. He assured me that this was the way it was to be. He said he would always be there for me. I immediately turned away and left the tunnel returning to where I had begun to travel and the voice said:

"Now you know it all. The understanding you have has been given. You will see the healer Prince today in Mamelodi. Tell him what you have seen. Know that much more will be shown as you need it to help others. But know that all you need to understand has been given. As it has been, and as it is and as it will always be, so be these things."

Further Encounters with Sangomas

That morning I went directly with Stan to visit Prince, the sangoma and prophet I had visited a year before. We immediately embraced and acknowledged how each of us had looked forward to this reunion. Prince commented that all had moved along very well and that my preparation had come to an end — the transition to becoming a healer was complete. He said I had the brain of an eagle. Since I had never told him anything about my association with the eagle, I was startled by how easily he had seen this. I told him the dream I had had and he acknowledged it was very true and powerful. He emphasized that I had to find those crocodile teeth during this trip. He went on to say that it was important to find the teeth as well as the skin of the crocodile. In addition, I needed to find the skin of a leopard, which is a complement to the crocodile. With those things my dreams and visions would become even stronger.

I was then taken to the back of Prince's home where he had a huge area on the ground covered with clay and symbolic drawings. He said all his ancestors lived there. I asked if I could sing for them and he invited me to do so. For the next twenty minutes, songs and chants came through me in honor of his ancestors. My hands began shaking and I applied them to Princes' body, working on his spine, heart, and head. I then bowed in front of this special place and kissed the soil. A man who had been working near the house came and asked to shake my hand. When I touched him I trembled and blessed him with energy. He said, "You have come to the right place. This is a good place to be."

Prince and I went off, and, after a long silence, he said, "You are a very powerful healer. You will be able to heal everything, including every bone in the body. Many famous people are going to come to you and you will be well known. You are not to fear this attention, but to accept it. As these things come, remember to pray even harder. This will keep you humble and good." He then talked about how the spirits were calling him to come to the United States. I told him about the vision of the four colors and how a Sioux medicine man had dreamed of four people coming together to make a prayer. I suggested we should each pray about whether he was the black stick in that vision. I believed he was and felt strongly he would visit the United States.

He spoke of how the spirits instructed him to cure many kinds of cancer. His work in that area had resulted in his being invited to London. A subsequent trip had been organized for him to visit Paris and other European cities, but the organization supporting it fell apart. His visions were showing him he would share his work in the United States rather than Europe. He was waiting for this to happen. Prince asked if I would stop and see him before I returned. He wanted to visit one more time. His last words that day were that I would make music that would spiritually reach and change many people.

Stan and I immediately drove to a Muti shop where herbs and traditional medicines are sold. I walked straight to a shelf and reached behind a row of jars, pulling out a jar of crocodile teeth. My hand had been led to them. When I inquired about the price, the woman behind the counter said she would have to call the "old man." Within minutes, an old sangoma entered and invited us to his home.

Located several miles from his shop, his home was filled with rooms of medicines, drums, skins, and other items related to his healing practice. He pulled out the whole skin of a crocodile, saying this is the one that belonged to the teeth. It was a large, man-eating-size crocodile. He asked what I wanted and, remembering my vision, I asked for the underneath skin that covered the stomach and for the top of the crocodile's head. An assistant came out and sawed off the pieces.

The sangoma invited us to look through his medicines and showed us a lion skin given to him by his grandfather. We then sat down and Stan asked to see his drums. I told the sangoma if he would play them I would bring forth a song. He instructed several of the women to play these drums. The second they started drumming, I went into a possession state, quickly jerking and shaking. Songs and chants started coming out and I placed my shaking hands on the sangoma.

As the drumming progressed and the singing escalated, one of the women began to become possessed. Her sounds escalated the intensity of the sounds coming out of me. Within minutes a spirit began speaking through me and I crawled into the little room the woman had entered. She and I both emitted a whole range of sounds and wild body movements. I became a leopard on all fours, wildly roaming through the area. I then sang and moved as an eagle and touched the woman next to me.

Muti shop where crocodile teeth were found

Someone removed my shirt and placed the crocodile belly skin over my stomach. I felt the crocodile was piercing and sucking my blood from my left breast and I shouted with further energy and frenzy. After about thirty minutes of absolute raw possession, the sangoma entered, saying, "Yes we have seen the great mamba in this man. Please spare his life and let him return." He did something to my fingers, arms, and neck, and I was awakened.

My whole body was wet with perspiration. My possession had involved being mounted by his ancestors, a snake, leopard, eagle, and Jesus, while my feet aggressively beat the floor as a drum. I perceived on some level that the power of this had frightened the sangoma. Stan later confirmed this and said he had to calm and assure him. The sangoma's wife also had become frightened. The other women, however, had fully opened to the experience.

After this episode, I shared some of my dreams with the sangoma. He said he had seen the spirits in me and that I should listen to these ancestors. He said that his home was always available for me to sleep in, eat in, or visit. When I left, his last words were, "From this moment on, we are the same. We are relatives." We embraced and I left with the crocodile skins and teeth.

On our way out, Stan heard him chuckling that his wife had never believed the things he was involved with until today when she saw what had happened. Stan and I left with a sense of amazement and felt even more bonded as spiritual brothers. He and I were complements to each other. His way was to be very still, calm, and peaceful, and my way was to amplify, transform, and project energy.

The next day, a doctoral student, Derek, came asking to discuss some things. He said he had worked at a job where the night watchman was a sangoma. Every night when the watchman finished his job, he would meet with him and listen to his stories. He was struggling with the pull of that other world and said he was having difficulty letting go and fully experiencing it.

After a talk about my experiences and visions, we parked in a shopping mall parking garage and I laid my hands on him, allowing the spirits to speak and sing. After a while, he began to chant. His hands trembled and his face changed. I applied energy to his fingers and continued the chanting. At the end of this work, I opened my eyes and saw a black South African policeman bending over the car staring into the front windshield. Behind us was a line of approximately twenty cars stopped, waiting to move. It was as if the world had paused for this moment to take place. Derek woke up, we got out of the car and went to a restaurant for lunch. He said I must meet the sangoma, Credo Mutwa, who may be the holiest man in Africa.

Zululand

The very next day, Peter, Ansie, and I took off to Zululand. On our way, Ansie described her own experience of healing as one of being brought more directly in contact with spirit. As a result, she had more faith in her spirituality. Her comment supports part of my own understanding of the process of healing. Shamans, or those shaken by the spirits, sacrifice their identity to be a vehicle for demonstrating the presence of spirit. Observing, touching, or hearing this feeds the faith of others. With a submission to this greater faith, one may be healed. The healer helps others have more faith through enacting a performance of his or her own faith.

The mission that we visited in Zululand was named Kwa Sizabantu, founded by the white Christian evangelist, Erol Stegen. We arrived late at night and en route were detained by a roadblock of policemen on a gravel road in the mountains. They were investigating everyone due to the violence in Zululand often involving several murders every day. The shiver of fear this encounter with the military brought forth was like a premonition of how I would experience Kwa Sizabantu.

When we entered the gates of the mission, I immediately felt dizzy and disoriented. Within minutes it was clear that this was a "corrupted" spiritual place. It didn't take long to recognize that its leaders were mostly white racists with an extremely judgemental, nonloving orientation to the people they were supposedly serving. The Zulu, a name meaning "people of the heavens," had been evangelized by these missionaries and had been empowered with the skills and technical knowledge of European engineering and agriscience. The place economically prospered with its successful harvests of vegetables, Kiwi fruit, dairy farming, and so forth.

The spiritual life of the mission, however, was without joy and humility. Zulus who did not subscribe to the official definition of "Christianity" were called "heathens." The man who was our host used the word "heathen" in almost every other sentence. I had to pray very hard to not get excessively angry at this man. At the same time it was necessary to address his spiritual and cultural racism. I finally asked him, "How is it possible to love someone with the love of Jesus if you call him a 'heathen?'" Startled, he went off on a discussion of liberal theologians not understanding that "heathen" simply means "not Christian."

Everywhere we were taken it was clear that there was only one accepted world view. Other spiritual practices were called witchcraft and evil and even "shaking" by so-called Christians was seen as related to the devil. Having heard enough, I challenged these people to consider that Jesus's way was marked by humility and service. They talked about bussing in outside Zulu children to interact with their "Christian children" and what a blessing that was to the (heathen) children. I asked if their children learned anything from their visitors and the response was, "How could they? They are violent people."

The whole experience at this mission in Zululand chilled me. I had traveled across the world with some apprehension and concern about meeting "sangomas" and "witchdoctors" and had eagerly anticipated meeting people serving in the path of Jesus. Surprisingly, I found the love of Jesus in the so-called "witchdoctors" and the dark absence of love in these Christians. How confusing the presence of good and evil can be.

The use of generalizations as a navigational guide through spiritual territory is often worthless. One must rely upon the compass bearing of one's heart to make decisions regarding how to encounter a particular spiritual offering. I felt love and made relatives with sangomas and felt disengaged and disgust in a Christian mission.

Rather than staying through the weekend at Zululand as had been arranged, I decided to leave the very first day. Thanking our hosts for their hospitality, I left them a letter acknowledging how they had brought practical skills to the Zulu people. I added, however, that I did not feel the presence of Christ's love and joy in their mission. Going on, the letter pointed out that the missionaries could learn a lot from these people if they would open their hearts to receive them as equal — equal in both the human and spiritual realms.

We immediately left what felt like a spiritual concentration camp. I became cognizant of how the place was an exaggerated version of what many churches, particularly white churches, are like in my own country. Christianity becomes an ideology pushed on people for the sake of helping the Christian feel spiritually important. Promising economic advantages and physical comfort, people trade their souls to a religious organization that does everything it can to kill spiritual experience. I began to realize the extent to which spiritual corruption has become quite comfortable in many Christian churches.

The image and life of Jesus must be kept distinct from this bastardization of His way. From that day on I decided I would sometimes refer to Him as Christ-Eagle. In this way, the form of how He was presented to me would be retained and any associations of Him with the corrupted practices of misaligned Christian churches would be avoided.

The Mother Sangoma

After our visit to Kwa Sizabanto, Stan took me to see Prince again. The other name Prince goes by is Mashimelo. Prince said he was expecting me and that he had seen me returning the night before. We went to where his ancestors were and this time my whole body began vibrating vertically, up and down. My hands went to Prince's body and the work was much stronger than it had been the previous time we were together. There were also spoken words given to him and sounds were sent into his body.

I told him he was the one to visit my country and join with three others to make a prayer. He said he knew this was so. His dreams also told him a trip to Botswana to meet the Bushmen was meant to happen and that it was good for me to go. He gave me some medicine for protection. He looked forward to the new changes I would bring back from Botswana.

Stan and I then went to visit another sangoma, a large black woman named Anna. To get to her, we went through rugged dirt paths, passing shanties made of plywood and tin. When we met her, Stan asked to be taken to the woman who was referred to as "the major source." More simply referred to as "the mother," she was the one other sangomas went to for direction. After waiting a while, I was summoned by Anna to come with her and meet the mother.

Walking along a steep path, we entered a dirt backyard where a large room was waiting with the mother sitting at one end. When I was introduced, our eyes froze on each other, and my arms shook when our hands met for greeting. Instantly she called for the drums and four or five drums were brought in along with other men and women.

When the drumming started, I quickly began vibrating and then joined with the singers, offering a chant that fit within their song. The mother sangoma immediately became frightened, left the room, and Stan had to go out to assure her that all was fine. When she came back, my possession increased to an absolute frenzy. I again became a leopard on all fours, growling at everyone. Following that, I was thrown on the floor as a mamba snake crawling around and through all the drummers.

I began speaking to everyone in another language and found I could understand what was being said. It was about the four directions of spirituality and the need for us all to come together. As I spoke they responded with affirmations and their own sounds. And then it was back again into the spirit creatures. My arms waved and I became the screeching eagle. The black hair of a wild animal was then put into my hands and I made it dance to the rhythms of the song. I placed it in my navel, crotch, heart, and mouth as well as waved it in all directions. I then felt I was crossing over into a place near death. I had never gone this far before and I immediately jumped up and, with eyes wide open, ran to every person in the room and touched them with shaking hands. Sometimes I would speak or chant in other languages to an individual. Following that, I bowed on the floor and sang several spirit songs.

During this time, my shirt and socks had been removed, and I was totally drenched with perspiration. I was asked to sit in a certain direction and a large wooden pot was placed on top of my head. A male sangoma and the mother sangoma bathed me with the liquid that was in it. It was very foul smelling, and, following my bath, a stick was put in my mouth that had foam in it. I was told to "eat." I swallowed and with each gulp a strong sound came forth. They told me this is always done for the spirits.

They sat me in a chair and I discovered a large cloth with guinea fowls all over it wrapped around me. The mother sangoma said I must find the same cloth and offer it to my grandfather. When I finally came to full consciousness, everyone said, "Good morning." I assumed this was a welcome back to life after visiting the other side.

Within a few minutes, the son of the mother sangoma became possessed and the spirit of his Grandmother spoke to him, saying something about one of my spirits coming from the bottom of a river or the sea. His Grandfather then spoke, saying that his ancestor was working with the ancestor of a white man in the area of mental health. He then danced wildly and ecstatically. Little did I know he had a foot injury that barely allowed him to walk. In his ecstasy he was dancing effortlessly.

Following his dancing I went to a separate room where the mother sangoma and Anna were sitting. The mother sangoma said I was welcome to visit anytime, and she would teach me anything she knew. She added it was important for me also to teach someone else about these ways. The ancestors told her it was important for me to go to Botswana. There was something there for me to receive.

I told her my vision about the origin of the four colors and that I was supposed to eat a mixture of black snake, crocodile blood, and yolk of the crocodile eggs. She was moved and immediately turned to her medicines and made this very mixture for me. I was told to eat it and that a new change would occur. She said that from now on the spirits and ancestors would ask for more things. I was to obey their requests and find them. In addition, the medicine I had taken would help the spirits speak. In this way I would provide a voice for them. Her final suggestion was to keep my faith in the Lord.

She asked me to visit her again and giggled about how our lives were the same. The two sangoma women made caricature body gestures of being possessed and we all laughed together. We then kissed and hugged each other. I told them I would see them again.

Stan and I left Mamelodi absolutely speechless. We had been overwhelmed by the amount of energy brought forth in the room. One person's eyeglasses had even cracked during this session. At one point I felt I had come up to the very edge of my own life — to take another step would be to die. Stan said everyone in the room had been brought to the edge of existence and the middle point between life and death breathed through the room. We then turned to laughing at the absurdity of two white men, Stan of Jewish background and me of Christian heritage, going into the homes of sangomas and bringing them the most energy they had ever witnessed. Rather than being ghostbusters, we were ghostmakers.

Mama Mona

I went home exhausted and found my right eye filled with pus. For some unknown reason I had developed an eye infection. Then it hit me that I was to visit Mama Mona Ndzekeli, the healer at Soweto the next morning.

Author with Mama Mona Ndzekali, Soweto

She was having serious medical trouble with her eyes. I wondered if my eye problem was related.

The night before visiting Mama Mona, I was awake most of the night. I prayed hard to Jesus and asked whether evil was to be in my body. I then was shown what I had seen at the sangoma mother's place the day before — a cross that alternated between being black and white. Although understanding had been given regarding the center point between good and evil, it went against everything I had been taught in the church. I knew on some level it was too late because I had accepted both good and evil into my being. My prayers aimed at asking to be used for good purposes.

That night, for the first time, I asked my grandfather what he wanted. He immediately said, "Get the whole hide of an otter, make it into a bag and tie the colored ribbon you've been shown into its nostril." He told me to ask my Midéwiwin friends to help find and prepare this.

I was then shown an image of a large tree in the Kalahari desert. If this tree was found, I was told to reach my hand into a hole in the tree. I was to pull out something that looked like larvae and eat it. I was to do this with absolute faith even though the hole might contain snakes and the larvae-looking substance might be poisonous.

When it came time to go to Soweto, I prayed and sang spiritual music, asking to be used as a tool for the spirits. I was afraid this woman might be a "Christian healer" who, despising evil, would recognize my spirits and tell me to get lost. At the same time, I felt called to touch her and heal her body. It should be noted that there is always a natural fear about going into Soweto. Sometimes dead bodies count on the road to Soweto alone is several dozen per day. Violence against white people is the norm and is expected. A week later I was warned not to enter Soweto again, because someone had threatened to kill me if I returned.

I prayed hard to be in the care of the spirits, allowing them to choose my life or death. When we arrived, Mama Mona's husband, Reverend L.F. Ndzekeli, was standing at the end of the driveway to greet us. His eyes and smile were a homecoming and all of us felt more at peace. As we entered their home, a prayer was uttered. My first look at Mama Mona felt like seeing a holy person. She had a very assuring, calming, and peaceful presence. Her husband said she had traveled throughout the world and it was clear to us that she was a great healer.

Afraid to tell her all my story, particularly the parts about my encounters with evil, I began telling the vision of climbing the spiritual ladder into the seven heavens. I then told her about how I flew as an eagle to her house and gave her the eagle's eyes and how my eye had been full of pus the night before. Before I could go on, she interrupted saying, "Your spirit guide is very, very strong. You are like me. The spirits took me everywhere and filled me with many dreams. Then I met a great healer who gave me one candle. After that time my life was given to healing others. I will now heal you and you will be ready."

She then got up from her chair and placed her hands all over my body, on my hands, arms, head, neck, back, solar plexus, legs, feet, and so forth. I began shaking and had to hold back from going into a wild frenzy. She groaned deeply, commenting on how strong my spirit guides were. She then gave me some hot water to drink with a spoon and spoke to me.

"You are very lucky. You have been chosen to be a great healer. The guides will tell you to get many things for them and you must do this. I see your grandmother surrounding you. She does not speak, but she is all around you. I now am going to give you all the spirit guides of Africa." She then got up and with her hands shot spirits into me. I continued to shake and could feel she was passing on some part of herself.

Following this she said she was very sick. I asked to touch her and she accepted. When I touched her, I felt love for her life. Jesus came into me, and her whole body was touched and shaken. A gentle, loving song was given, and some sounds shot into her back. More aggressive sounds came out when I worked with her leg. Finally I held her, and every joint in my body shook her.

Afterwards she said, "You have healed me. I have seen the spirit of Jesus working through you." She then said, "You must go to the church and pray your heart out at the altar." Her husband, the pastor of the church named "Inkonzo Yabaphilisi Soweto Spiritual Church," took us immediately. While kneeling at the altar I again saw the cross going back and forth between being black and white. I prayed very hard to be rid of self and to be used by the spirits for the good of all people.

The Reverend Ndzekeli then explained that the church was for healers. Healers from all over the world had found their way to it. The church banner had the word "Ekuthuleni" meaning "place of quiet." Healers came here to find quiet and be taught by Mama Mona. Reverend Ndzekeli told me again how lucky I was and that my life was just like that of Mama Mona. He said, "You now have all the spirit guides of Africa in you."

I walked around the church and was led to three small stones and two feathers. The one feather, a small white one, I placed in my shirt pocket over my heart. When it was picked up, a voice said, "Give this to Ansie." I decided to wait to see if this was for her. The other feather and three stones I placed in the left pocket of my pants. During the drive home, a voice shouted, "Give Ansie the feather now!" I immediately gave it to her.

Several days before, she and I had walked together in the woods where I placed my hands on her and we shook together. The next day I asked her to paint a picture of my vision of the cloud next to the waterfall. That evening she had an extremely vivid dream of entering a cave inside of which she was shown the tree of life. A leaf fell from the tree and landed in her hand, turning into a beautiful white and black bird. That bird immediately turned into hundreds of smaller birds that flew away. When I gave Ansie the feather she said it belonged to the bird she saw in her dream. Furthermore, in the sunlight it looked like the leaf that fell from the tree of life.

Mama Mona and her husband repeatedly thanked Peter and Ansie for bringing me to them. They said the spirits would bless their home for doing this. When we went back to Mama Mona's home after visiting the church, her husband told us about how Mama Mona once had to walk through a swamp up to her neck with many crocodiles all around her. If she panicked, she was told she would die. Her body received many spirits and her main spirit guide was Sister Elize, a Mother Superior who had passed over in the past.

When Mama Mona was a child, she had many visions, particularly of being surrounded by very small babies with wings. The spirit world was filled with celestial music that vibrated her very core. She was taken through rocks, streams, and mountains. All through her life she often has been surrounded by a visible fog. Through praying for others and specifically for her own spiritual development, she developed into an internationally acclaimed healer, with many records substantiating her work.

When Sister Elize sends messages to Mama Mona, they are in the form of specific tasks for people. These interventions reminded me of what I tell clients to do in therapy sessions. Sister Elize may tell someone to purchase a blue cape and wear it to church or buy tobacco and have someone puff some smoke saying, "I am smoking this on behalf of so-and-so who is already in spirit." In another case, she had someone purchase a handkerchief and then, after blessing it, had it sent to an ailing aunt.

Whereas a faith healer helps someone save himself through his own belief, a "medium" can use many methods to heal independently of the person's belief. Mama Mona described herself and me as mediums who are used by the spirits in many different ways to heal. She summarized the process as "love conquering all." Warning people against their own tempers and dark moods, she advises us to cleanse our minds so that the holy spirit may pour in.

The vibrations and power of a healer are raised with music, singing, and dancing. The rhythms of jazz particularly attract spirits, she noted. Mama Mona came from a family of musicians and agrees that music is a main door for reaching the spirit world.

She and her husband predicted many unexplainable things would happen to me and that the rest of the world would never be able to understand it. I then decided to tell her of the vision I had of the earth's origin and of the black snake in my belly. I decided it was time to tell everything. She and her husband welcomed this revelation and said, yes, both evil and good must be in you. They gave me almost exactly the same explanation that had previously come to me of standing in the middle of evil and good and of not being indulgent in either side. We talked about this more and more, and all that had happened to me was fully confirmed. I became healed at that moment and knew that I must always trust what the spirits tell me, no matter how strange or different it may seem. Reverend Ndzekeli introduced me to others throughout the day as, "the great healer."

Mama Mona said that the spirits told her to give me a candle to take home to the United States. When I got home, I was to light it in the evening and let it burn through the entire night. She also said I needed to offer some silver coins to the sea or river that is next to the city where I was born. I later recalled the sangoma the day before had been told by an ancestor that I was connected to a spirit under the sea or river. Within twenty-four hours, the spiritual visions of two different healers had overlapped. When I thought of the river next to where I was born, I realized I was born near the banks of the Mississippi River and that I was presently living about six hundred miles north of my birth place near the banks of the very same river.

She said the guides will tell you everything you need to know in the future. She acknowledged the strength of the Bushman's guides and noted it was good for me to go there. After visiting them, she advised going somewhere and sitting still and being quiet. Peter had planned for us to go to the Okavanga Delta immediately after the Kalahari and be dropped off on an isolated island where we would be still.

Amazingly, every day of my trip to Africa was the reception of a new piece of the shamanic puzzle, each piece given exactly at the right time, place, and sequence. Meeting Mama Mona and her husband confirmed that I was being born into a new life. Peter, Ansie, and I all acknowledged how holy the day had been. We all had been brought together for spiritual work, and we felt our lives would never be the same again.

When we got back to Peter and Ansie's home, I looked at the letterhead Reverend Ndzekeli gave me with their phone number on it. On this letterhead were drawn three seven-sided-circular-like figures with a symbol inside each. The northern symbol was that of a black cross. It was inside the largest circle. Connected to it to the west in a smaller circle was a rooster and to the east was connected a circle containing a barrel. I then noticed the three stones I picked up consisted of one large white stone with a black cross on it and two smaller stones, one with a barrel and the other with the head of a rooster. The feather I found was a rooster feather, black with a white edge. I lay down and knew I had to tell Mama Mona this.

I called her and when I told her about the stones, she yelled out a scream of acknowledgement. She had used these three white stones to heal and they had been taken away. A spirit guide said the stones would return someday. She said, "You are very lucky. The spirits are bringing you good luck."

Somehow I knew the cross of Jesus was a main source of spiritual energy for Mama Mona and that it alternated between black and white, evil and good. The barrel contained the water she sometimes gives people after she touches them. As I wondered about the chicken, an egg was dropped in the Johnson's kitchen, spilling yolk over the floor. The eggs of these chickens, specifically the yolk, must be somehow connected to her work, perhaps along with the chicken's blood. All of these things were revealed and with these understandings, Mama Mona and I were being united.

Kalahari

The night before our trip to the Kalahari, I took the medicine Prince had given me for protection. Going to a quiet place outside, I broke the stem as he had instructed, made a prayer to be led safely to where we were supposed to go, and then lit it with a match so the smoke could be inhaled. As the medicine smoked, two orange, glowing circles appeared in it like two eyes. The two orange circles disappeared and became one orange circle that looked like the moon. I had to blow on it to see if it was from the fire or whether I was hallucinating. As I allowed myself to focus on it singularly, the orange moon became two, then one, then two. At that moment I heard the sound of an owl calling. I went to tell Peter. He said the owl was in the front yard on top of a lamp pole. He added that if you shine a light on the owl, its eyes will appear orange.

It was clear that the time had come for this trip, this full baptism into the spirit world, where I would be put to death and rise into a new life. My journey into the Kalahari was sent with prayers and blessings by North American medicine men, the pastor, deacons, and the congregation of New Salem, and the sangomas and healers from Africa. My body, mind, heart, and soul had become full of the spirits and all tunings and preparations had taken place. The journey was set to go. It was my last night in the world to which I always had been accustomed. When I returned, and I believed I would, the crossover would be complete. The spirits and guides were ready for me, and I had done all I knew to be ready for them. I was ready to die and be reborn to walk a life as a healer and spiritual guide for others.

Mama Mona had mentioned several times that the Buddha would soon come to me. I subsequently wondered whether "Mahari," a name given to me months before by the spirits, was the name of a spirit guide associated with the Buddha. Only time would tell. A word in Botswana that sounds similar to "Mahari" means "at home" or "we are still at home." Whatever the case, "Mahari" was the name of a voice coming in the future.

The night before taking off to Botswana, many spirit creatures came to me in my dreams. It was as if the entire jungle were alive and present in my mind's eye. In addition to the creatures, I saw a large room filled with hundreds of masks. A beautiful young woman's face and head without hair also appeared. At first I was startled until I realized that long ago nuns shaved the hair off their head. I knew this must be Sister Elize. Only her head and neck were visible and around her neck was a necklace of seven stars, the same white stars I had seen associated with healing and with Jesus. As I stared at these stars, a second necklace came out of them, as if newly born from the original one. This necklace lifted up, hovered over her head, and then came down over my head. The next morning Sister Elize came back and said, "You and I are to unite. We are to be wed as one." She later said, "We are to be married." Hearing that was most startling, to say the least. How could I marry a spirit, let alone a spirit nun? If that wasn't enough, it was revealed that Sister Elize was herself connected to the Virgin Mary and that somehow Mary, through her, and Jesus, who lives in my heart, would become one again.

Before heading off to the Kalahari, Ansie promised to paint a picture of my vision of the waterfall while we were gone. With this last detail in place, Peter and I took off for Botswana. Although Alec Campbell, the former director of the National Museum of Botswana, had given us several suggestions where to go, I saw the place in a vision. It was all the way to the edge of the central Kalahari. Going past Molepolole, Letlhakeng Khudumelapswe, Salajwe, and Khunaware, we traversed difficult, sandy paths, having to stop several times to either get unstuck or rearrange supplies. When we went past the point where we no longer had enough fuel to return, I said we must go on because the vision showed this to be our destination. I assumed the spirits would guide, protect, and give us fuel. Within minutes of getting to the interior of the Kalahari, a large, beautiful black and white eagle, a ntaga eagle, appeared in front of our vehicle.

This eagle arrived directly in front of us at the very moment I saw my first Bushman in front of a hut. We instantly went to the hut and out came the chief elder accompanied by another man. The other man came up to me and held out his two palms toward my face. My palms went into his palms and began shaking. We then hugged and I vibrated his back. He gave an exclamation of joy and my heart felt at home. I greeted, hugged, and vibrated the chief elder, Mantaga. He smiled and his first words were, "I have been sick all year and you have come. I believe you have healed me." I told him I had come from across the world to visit them and that my spirit guides had brought me. He said this was good. I asked if he would grant permission for me to participate in their dance. He said he would call the people together and dance that night. Women and children then arrived and I hugged them, giving each a vibration. They all knew what it was — it was their way of healing. Smiles, laughter, and joy were in the air. I was beginning to realize the gift the Bushmen were giving me was their complete acceptance of me as a healer. They would be the ones who would ceremonially bury my old self and bring to life my rebirth as a fully committed healer. Dancing with them would be the ritual for this transformation.

In the afternoon prior to the dance, a very old man came by to visit. We asked him about healing, and he said he sometimes does this, particularly sucking away disease. He said the spirits taught him to do it. After this chat I touched him, vibrating his back and chest. In return he touched my chest and shoulders, appeared to remove something, and then spat it away. Without any translator to provide a text, we shared a pristine moment of healing. This very moment had taken place over and over since the beginning of time. These people, the Bushmen of Africa, may have been the first to receive this gift. In touching them and in being touched by them, I felt connected to the very beginning of healing practices.

As the sun began to go down, Bushmen began arriving in front of our camp. We had been invited by the chief to live with them, and we set up our tent under a large Camelthorn tree. Men, women, and children arrived, bringing with them pieces of bushes and tree limbs for the great fire they would build. They were teasing each other and light humor filled the air.

As it became dark, the fire began to get stronger and some of the men danced a few steps outside the circle. With more and more songs, the power of the dance began to get into everyone's bones. A healer brought out a cerval skin (a wild cat) and spoke to it. He made several consultations with some of the people, and the dance went on. The set up involved a large fire, with women and children circling it. Men would dance around the women and sometimes enter the ring to dance immediately next to the fire. When the healer went inside the circle, he carried and waved a wisk made of a wild animal's tail.

Soon other men began seriously dancing inside and outside the circle, and everyone felt the increasing power. Before I knew it, my whole body began shaking, particularly my legs. They were trembling in convulsion-like fashion. I then began stomping the ground hard and dancing with shaking legs. Two men came close to me and I joined in the dance with them. And then the most extraordinary heat filled my belly. It felt like the fire inside the circle was inside my belly. No other part of my body had this heat.

As the dance moved on, I began to groan and allow sound to come out. As if some invisible signal had been given, two other men and I began putting our hands on everyone — children, women, and men. As I touched them, I trembled, shook, and gave off wailing sounds. Although it was different for each person, my hands typically worked with their heart, throat, back, and heads. When I started to pass out, I would back off and dance more. The other healers would help hold me up and we would hold each other's hands and shake. I never had felt this form of bonding in a ceremony before.

The dance went on and on, and I found myself going in and out of its power. At a point when I thought I was going out of it, my legs began trembling and vibrating more wildly than I have ever felt them move in my life. They were in synch with the polyrhthyms and sounds of the dance. Several Bushmen began pointing and laughing with joy at the sight of a white man starting to really get the dance into his body. And then it happened: without any effort, the dance danced me. I cannot fully explain this, but the power got into my hips, energizing my feet and legs to have a life of their own. All the bushmen immediately noticed, smiled with approval, and clasped their hands with joy. The combination of peace, calm, and raw power this dance brought on was remarkable. It pushes one deeper into its own energy.

I danced and danced until a group of people came running toward me. One man grabbed me and my mind knew that an emergency had occurred and I was being asked to help. At that moment I existentially died. I was no longer who I was and immediately became fully taken over by the spirits. Speaking in another language, I went around the circle and, on the other side, found a man on the ground who looked like he was dead. They took me to him and, with my whole body and deep chanting, I brought him back to consciousness. We then embraced and put our foreheads together. The shaking of our heads danced together, and I felt my fingertips going into his head.

Later an elder man looked into my eyes and I felt a love embracing all of humanity. We immediately embraced and his hot hands went to my back. The shaking was very strong, and we were both going into a deeper place. Another healer ran to us and threw us to the ground. All three of us were on top of each other shaking, vibrating, and moaning. We were giving our lives to heal one another.

I knew from the moment the dance began to get into me that this was the ritual of transformation my dreams had sent me to receive. I didn't have to ask permission to dance, the dance chose me to dance it. Without being able to understand any of their language, we had all fully understood what had taken place. The spirits had filled us with boiling life energy that was shared freely with everyone. The healing was both created and received from the power binding everyone together around the fire.

Not only had the dance gotten into my bones, but my body had healed and been healed by these people. After I was called by the community to heal someone who had "died," there was no doubt that these people had helped me be reborn as a healer who had no doubts as to his shamanic calling. This was no longer who I was to become, this was who I am.

The dance lasted until the fire went out. We all departed by giving gestures of thanks and love through clasped hands and full eyes. It was a night that would never be forgotten. Peter spoke of it as one of the most incredible experiences of his life. Here we were in the central Kalahari under a canopy of blazing stars dancing the healing dance with the Bushmen around a fire in the middle of the community and in the middle of the belly. This was a place to die and become reborn.

The next morning I took sand from all around the circle both inside and outside where the singers had been seated. I wanted to take this sand as a remembrance of my new life. I also took away some of the ashes of the fire as ashes from the burning away of my past life.

We stayed on to learn more about these people's lives. On the first day we were with the Bushmen, the spirits told me I would meet a man named Twele, who would help us. As it turned out, Twele was our Bushmen guide to the people in the village. His father was the old healer who visited us. He also made me a necklace from gemsbock gut for my crocodile teeth.

On the morning after the dance, Twele and the chief came to us and the old man thanked me for using my hands to heal the community. He said I had blessed their people because they were now talking and being together more. He also said he knew I would heal his sickness. The people were talking about what I had done with my "holy hands" at the dance.

I asked where the healing dance came from, and he said it was a gift from the spirits. Although it was given to the people of the Kalahari desert, he said I had permission to take the dance with me. He said the spirits continue to come and give people unique variations of the dance. I told him who some of my spirit guides were and the vision I had had about the creation of the world's peoples. He thanked me for giving him this vision and said I had come here to find my home. He pointed to a tree and

Twele, Bushman guide in Central Kalahari

Home in the Kalahari

said that was my home, and I could be there anytime I wanted. Furthermore, he implied my soul would return there when I died. We talked about the need for different people to come together. He agreed that if the four colors of people do not dance and pray together, then the world will end. He said we must cooperate with one another to survive.

I told him about the origin of the pipe with the red-skinned people who were the first people on the land where I lived. In explaining the gift of the White Buffalo Calf Woman, the spiritual function of the pipe was given. I then gave him a pipe I had received from Pipestone, Minnesota, the quarry where the pipes are made. This pipe had been smoked by me, and I had seen a light around its stem one night. He was deeply moved and said that he and the community would be strongly blessed by this gift. He believed it would help save their people.

He then showed us around the community, introducing us to the various thatch homes surrounded by thorn bushes to keep out the lions. Along the way I asked him, for no apparent reason at the time, the significance of the deiker horn. He said it was holy and worn around the neck of men who lift it on top of their heads while doing the healing dance. Within an hour, Peter and I found a deiker horn in the sand and Twele immediately made it into a necklace.

The tree that marked my home was facing another tree with an eagle's nest. Without a doubt, I knew this was my first spiritual home. This is where the healing practice that came to me was originally born. Looking up to the sky at the moment of this realization were three black and white eagles.

In the afternoon, I set out on a walk by myself to find the tree I had seen in a previous dream. Just beyond visual range of our camp, I saw a tree half of which looked like a snake coiling up into the sky. It had to be the tree. I could feel it drawing me toward it. When I got there I circled it and found a perfect hole exactly half way up the tree. I took a stick to see if anything alive was in it. It was too dark and deep to know. I then reached in and felt sand, but out came a small piece of something dark like a worm. Upon closer examination it was actually the core or "heart wood" of the tree, the part that carries water from the ground to give the tree life.

How appropriate it was to eat the center or heart of the tree in an area that was the first home for all healers! What I ate was the part that carried the healing water giving life. When I approached the tree, a small bird's feather fell from the sky in front of it. This was an absolute confirmation of the tree's being the one I was to find. I ate the core and knew that this land, water, tree, and life were now inside of me.

The night before we left, I went to the chief elder and gave him food, money for the children, and money to purchase two goats for their community. They were deeply moved by these gifts and held their hands over their hearts and then moved them toward me to express their appreciation and love. The chief elder asked for more healing, and we went to his home to perform a ceremony. Some elder women came, and one began singing the healing dance song. I went into the dance and worked with each of them. At the end, thanks were given for making us feel like home. I said I would try to see them again next year. The chief elder replied, "we will cook a Kudu as a feast next time."

On our last morning before departing, some of the village people came to say goodbye. They took us to Mantaga, the chief elder who had most of the other elders with him. They asked to be touched and healed one more time. Mantaga took off his shirt and I began to work very intensely on him. He and I stood and shook together in the rhythms of the dance. I had felt pain in my left shoulder and legs all night and went to work on those areas. Almost every member of the community came to be healed. I worked on them one by one, including the children. Often, my entire body shook their entire bodies. When I thought I would collapse from exhaustion, the old women would sing and begin to dance the healing dance. My feet would begin to dance and this was energizing. When the man who had previously "died" in the healing dance came to me, a huge amount of energy gathered and I danced toward him, picked him up in the air, and shook his whole body with the shaking of every bone in me.

The people were clapping and clasping their hands to their heart when the elder told us he would see us next year. His final words were, "You have healed me. You have healed the community. You have shown us it can be good to be with white people. It is now necessary for us to cooperate together. We wish you a safe journey." Still worked up from the healing, I went to the eldest woman. She seemed to carry the very heart and soul of the community. We embraced, shook together, and with my hands on my heart, I moved them to cover her heart. She and I then sang together.

I went down on my knees in front of Mantaga, the chief elder, and, speaking in tongues, I told them of their importance to the world and for the necessity of people of different colors to make dance and prayers together. I circled my hands through all the directions and finished with a song that expressed my love for them. He replied, "This is a blessing. This is very good."

As I walked away, the old woman came to me again, but this time with a baby in her arms. The three of us touched heads together, shook a dance, and sang from our hearts. I have never felt more connected. We had exchanged the most basic life force known. As we drove away, I felt fulfilled having found my first spiritual home, the place where healing had begun. These people and that place will be in my heart forever.

Several kilometers down the road, the spirits told me that if I saw a large bird, it would be a sign that everything that happened was true and that my life ahead would be one of offering healings and blessings for others. Within minutes, an enormous "secretary" bird flew over the car. This bird is given its name due to the feather stuck in its head that looks like a pen. This was a blessing to continue writing the story of my shamanic journey. The other interesting thing about the bird is that it feeds on poisonous snakes. It catches snakes, lifts them high into the air, and then drops them, killing them so they may be easily eaten. The secretary bird, the only terrestrial eagle in the world, like me, had a pen associated with its head and carried a snake in its belly. I was later to learn that early Bushmen had drawn the secretary bird on rocks to depict a shaman in avian form.

As we headed for the Okavango Delta, I recalled an experience that took place one night in the Kalahari. One evening we all sat in silence watching the stars. I decided to search for the star that felt like it was my own personal star. Near the southern cross I found it. In the absolute center of what first seemed a gigantic black cross bordered by a stretch of stars, it appeared to have a halo of light around it. As I looked more closely, this dark cross was actually the figure of a person.

The star in the center of this person and cross became my star. When I stared at it, it would blink and sometimes move. I heard a very quiet voice say it was the home of a spirit guide. I retired to my sleeping bag yet continued to look at it. What happened next is very difficult to explain. A tunnel appeared stretching from the star to me. It was instantly very perceptible and I felt hooked up to the star. Some outside animal then walked by, perhaps a dog, and I was distracted from seeing this tunnel. When I got back to the star again, it moved toward me, until it became a light in a nearby tree. Again, an animal distracted me. I finally went to sleep marveling on how close one can get to a star. The star and I had started some kind of relationship. Only the future would reveal how it was to play a part in my life.

Another event took place in the Kalahari that I have saved for mentioning last. On the last morning, at sunrise, I was again called to the tree with the hole in its side. As I approached, I noticed how it had two very distinct sides. On its left was the snake coiling up toward the sky that breathed a sense of death. On the right side was a completely different tree full of life with the hole in its center. I was told to go again to the hole and place my entire face into it. Closing my eyes, I did this and sang a song. Immediately I was shown the image of a man from India named "Mahari." He said, "Open your mouth and I will speak." I opened my mouth and began speaking for Mahari with an Indian accent.

He told me the spirits were aware of the many sacrifices and hardships I had made and they were very pleased. They had chosen to give me all the spirit guides on the condition I would continue to pray to be used as a vehicle for healing. Mahari said all things will be shown, and he promised to show me the Buddha soon. Wearing a white turban and having a light voice with warm humor, he even made up some ridiculous poems. He said he was the first of many guides like himself to come.

When we finally left the Bushmen and the secretary bird, I kept thinking about the tree and the voice of Mahari. This was the opening the mother sangoma in Mamelodi had said would take place. In the African world view, I had become a medium, a voice for Mahari and other guides that would appear later.

Author in central Kalahari

About two hours drive away from our tree with the Bushmen, Mahari came and said, "Close your eyes now." When I did, ten enormous fingers of two hands came out of the earth looking like the blossoming of a flower in fast motion photography. They were long, beautiful fingers belonging to the hands of someone from India. They formed a bowl-like structure, again looking like the petals of a flower, and out of it was born a volcano with what appeared as a womb on top. Inside this womb of fire, the great Buddha came forth. He simply said, "I have come to be with you." I then saw the Buddha retract into the volcano, which in turn went back inside the flower of finger petals. Finally, the hands went through my belly button and rested inside me.

It then came out of my belly button again —finger-flower-volcano and the Buddha. This time the Buddha had the black snake that was in my belly neatly wrapped around him. He said, "Now the energy of the snake can be focused by my singular vision." He then went back into my belly. The third time my navel opened, a tree came out indicating the Buddha had taken the form of a tree.

"There Is a Pipe in Guadalupe"

Later while traveling through the Okavanga in a Makura, the wooden canoe propelled by a tribesman with a long stick, I became very quiet, both on the inside and outside. I was told many dreams would take place that night and, as a matter of fact I awoke almost every hour with a dream. It began with being told that I would be "unwrapped." Then I saw myself looking somewhat like a mummy with rolls and rolls of cloth or tissue-like wrappings being removed. This was followed by a series of dreams removing old associations, uncertainties, and excess emotional baggage. After those dreams, I looked down at one side of my abdomen and found a large hole with pieces of bone and muscle showing. There was no blood and my insides were gone. I then realized I had been an egg shell and had cracked, releasing something from within. I was told I was now spiritually naked.

The next dream was the most dramatic, and, although its description may not express its intensity, it felt as powerful as the landing of a space-ship. The scene of the dream was in a car traveling at night through the desert. My sister Jan was driving the car and her son Jason was in the backseat with me. All of a sudden we were talking with a nun in full habit sitting on the passenger side of the front seat. I don't remember any of the conversation except for her last statement, "There is a pipe in Guadalupe." She then disappeared into thin air, and we were stunned because we had all seen and heard this nun. We went on and on about how we each couldn't be dreaming it. I then woke up thinking about this dream that was wondering about itself.

Sometime during the night, a tremendous amount of noise, sounding like a storm, woke me up. When I looked outside, a long, narrow, ghost-like white cloud came sailing toward the tent, entered it with an extreme chill, and moved right out. At that point I had my final dream; in it I was taken as a small boy to an upstairs bedroom. It was evening and I looked outside the window and saw the star I had seen in the Kalahari. Sister Elize spoke, saying, "This is where I am from." I am unable to remember what else she said.

Prior to leaving the Okavanga, we had a terrifying encounter with a herd of elephants. Our guide mistakenly got us too close to the elephants, who were peacefully grazing. Without warning, they turned and, with a great thunderous, trumpeting sound, began charging us. There was no where to run and nothing we could do. As we froze and faced these gigantic creatures, waves of adrenalin flushed through my whole body. At first I felt absolute fear, but this quickly turned to an exhilarating excite-ment, an enthusiasm about experiencing the very center point that holds the difference between life and death. In that moment I knew it would be an honorable death at the hands of nature. At the last instant the charging elephants turned, returning our life to us.

On our return trip, we decided to stay overnight in Francistown, Botswana. We pulled into a street where we discovered a shop responsible for tanning and distributing all game hides for the entire nation. I asked for a piece of leopard skin, and the manager came and asked what my purpose with it was. I explained I had traveled very far to get it for a healer. He then asked if I was this healer. When I told him I was, he asked if I would give him some medicine. We went to an isolated place and I touched him, sending so much energy into him it made us both dizzy. He wanted to know what I charged for healing, and I said I accept any gift that might be offered. He wanted me to see his friends and family members, but we had to move on.

Within minutes, he came out of the store room with most of a whole leopard skin. On the way out he also gave me the feather of the bataleur eagle. He said he had found many hides and special items for sangomas. Giving me his fax and phone number, he said he would get me whatever I needed in the future. He made me promise to let him know in advance when I would be in the area again. He wanted to gather some people for me to heal. Peter and I left his shop, utterly amazed at how we found what I was looking for.

When we returned from Botswana, Ansie had completed two paintings of the waterfall I had seen in my vision. She struggled for days over how to paint it, and, in a moment she described as a great burst of energy, the paintings came forth. They were the birth of her own style, a way of painting she had never accomplished before. When she took them to her teacher, the teacher wept, saying she had broken through into discovering herself.

During this time, the image of Jesus and the cross often came to me. I saw the cross as the whole pattern organizing one's relationship to the spirit world. Like Jesus, one should be stretched across all polarities, including good and evil. In this way, Jesus accepted our sins rather than negating or destroying them.

Healing, too, is not about eradication of evil, sin, sickness, illness, or pathology. It is about embracing sickness as a corner of the cross one carries. Accepting it as part of this sacred whole carries with it a resignation of one's individual will and surrender to the greater purpose of the Greater Spirit. Healing involves the recontextualization of a person into the sacred context, placing them in the middle of the four corners of the cross. Within the sacred, holy, or whole of the cross, a person becomes healed, that is, made one with the Great One. Here, the particular outcome of one's life is less relevant. One is ready to live and ready to die. At this point in the center of the universe, it is always a good day to die and a good day to live.

My own story of becoming a healer has been largely driven by ignorance. My lack of knowing freed me from the constraints of spiritual schools and traditions. In learning to be open and encumbered with few constraints, I found myself taken to the very beginning of healing, the shaking of the African Bushman.

The healing touch of life is available everywhere, yet almost everyone is blind to recognizing it. Following the trip to the Kalahari, Peter and I visited the Museum of South African Rock Art in Johannesburg. Eighty-nine rock petroglyphs or rock engravings are exhibited in an outdoor area demonstrating the "art" of the Bushmen. One of the engravings, number 21 taken from the Viljven Site 1, Kerksdorp, Transvaal, has the following descriptive note (Hilary J. Bruce, *The Museum of South African Rock Art : A Descriptive Guide*, Johannesburg Africanna Museum, 1982, p.141), "Man carrying bows and arrows, though thought by others to be a woman with a baby on her back and carrying a digging stick."

When I saw the figure, it was clear that it was a person holding another person with his hands for the purpose of healing. It was to me the clearest petroglyph in the entire collection. Calling over the supervisor of the museum, I pointed out this interpretation and he immediately agreed saying, "Yes, you are right." One of the most basic truths of the Bushman's life and of our own lives could not be seen when it was drawn clearly on a rock!

Credo Mutwa

Following the visit to these Bushman rock engravings, a trip was arranged in June, 1992, to meet Vusamazulu Credo Mutwa, the distinguished author of *Indaba My Children* and easily the most internationally known Zulu sanusi or medicine man. Living in a settlement in Mafikeng, Bophuthatswana, near the Botswana border, his life story is one of the most amazing tales of our time.

His grandfather, Ziko Shezi, was a High Witchdoctor, custodian of the Zulu relics and tribal history. Credo grew up as his attendant, carrying his medicine bags and being shown many secrets. He became a sculptor and then traveled widely through his country. Trained as a medicine man, he assumed his grandfather's post as Guardian of Tribal History and Custo-

Credo Mutwa conducting divination ritual with Sangomas

Credo Mutwa dancing with Sangomas

Credo Mutwa

Credo Mutwa conducting divination ritual with Sangomas

dian of the Sacred Tribal Relics. Mutwa is the spiritual leader of the sanusis, inyangas and sangomas, that is, the various types of healers throughout Africa and, as such, is recognized as the spiritual leader for millions of Black Africans.

In 1960, his fiance died when South African police fired on a crowd. On the night before her burial, he cut a vein in his left hand and took the "Chief's Great Blood Oath," swearing to tell the world the spiritual truths of his people even if it meant "imprisonment, torture or death, and even if the very fires of hell or the cold of Eternal Darkness stood in my way." The beginning of that path was his book, *Indaba* ("Speak") *My Children*, regarded by some critics as one of the most important literary works of Africa. Critics claimed "he is certainly the most astonishing writer so far produced by Africa" and that he "may be destined to become the most famous African of all time." Following the book's publication, his life involved more suffering. Mobs of hundreds surrounded his home when he lived in Soweto, swearing to kill him when he denounced the violence of his people and encouraged them to return to the old spiritual ways. He was stoned and rendered unconscious, one of the three times in his life he was pronounced "clinically dead."

Now an old man struggling with disease, he said he wanted to talk to me about how the death of the earth is related to the ever increasing problems that face psychotherapists. Most of my career had been focused on arguing how the lack of an "ecological" and "systemic" way of knowing and living was responsible for the many muddles people get themselves into, ranging from pollution of the ocean to violence in relationships. Perhaps I was going to a major leader of African healers to find that the ending of this chapter of my life was a return to where I had begun.

Credo Mutwa's home exists in a dreamscape. Surrounded by medicine wheels, sacred stones, large sculptures, skulls, petroglyph designs, art work, and spiritual renderings, he has created a place where his soul speaks directly in the outer world. Derek, the doctoral student whose spiritual door had been recently opened, set up the meeting with Credo. His wife, an artist, was a friend of an Austrian filmmaker who, on a dream, sold all her possessions and came to Africa to make a documentary partly focusing on Credo's life. This filmmaker gave us the address of Credo, and we drove to his home. On the way, Derek talked about how his life had radically changed since our healing encounter. Medicine dreams were coming to him as well as chanting and shamanic body movements. It was clear we were becoming spiritual brothers, and he was crossing into the territory of receiving the call to be a sangoma.

When we arrived at Credo's home, the community living with him greeted us. In addition to his family, there were residential sangomas in training. Although Derek told them we had an appointment, they replied he was sick and could not see anyone. I then spoke to his wife, a sangoma, saying, "I have come here from the United States because of a dream. I bring a sacred gift and a message." Instantly we were taken to see Credo Mutwa.

Sitting in a little shed he was covered with cloths of many designs. His presence was so strong, I had difficulty seeing his face, which often appeared as a fuzzy cloud. We shook hands and I immediately told him that the spirits had brought me to Africa to find my spiritual home with the Bushmen, by whom I was now adopted as a healer. I told him I had been instructed to bring a sacred pipe to give to a particular Bushman. While in the Kalahari, I gave my own pipe away because the spirits told me not to give up the other one. That pipe would be going to someone else. I told Credo that I now knew the pipe was for him, and that I was confused because the spirits told me it was going to a Bushman. I also acknowledged I felt his pain in my lungs and that I had come to touch him with my hands. Lastly, I told him the spirits told me to make one request, "Please teach me how to die."

His first words were, "My name, Mutwa means 'Bushman.' My grandfather, my mother's father, was a Bushman. I am a direct descendant of the Bushmen." He then received the pipe, held it in all the directions, and said, "The pipe is the earth, the smoke connects us with the spirit world, and the stem is the spine joining it to us." I voiced an Indian chant and a ceremony was created.

He subsequently asked his wife to give me her beads, saying, "I am wishing that the mother of my children will place this necklace, which is one of her necklaces, around your neck. It is made of a very sacred wood, the wood of purity. When a king passes away, this wood is burned. When a person is looking for the truth, this wood is burnt and a prayer is made around it. This wood is a protector." He then explained the origin of the blue and white beads and its relationship to being a sangoma. The necklace was placed around me in a ceremony that marked my initiation as a sangoma.

He then asked me to touch him. Holding his left hand with my left hand, my right hand vibrated and shook the rest of his body. I pointed to where his pains were and then sang into them. Following this healing work, he asked his wife to go tell the other sangomas that the sangoma from america had recognized his pains. He then said, "I will tell you a story; I want to tell you a story, a very strange story. I will tell the story, then I will stop, and then I will tell the story again. I will see how your spirits feel about it. First there was a man who had a son. This man was a man of God. He had many Bibles in his house. He lived on a farm, a small farm, and it was a good farm. It was far away in the land of the people of america. One day the man said to his son, 'My son, we need to talk.' The man took two pieces of cloth, a gray cloth and a dark blue cloth. Because he was a man of God and he could see very far away, he said, 'My son, this afternoon you have come down from the mountain where you always like to stay. I don't know what you do up there, but if my suspicion is correct, you rascal you, you are friends with some of the red Indian people.' The young man said, 'Father, your eyes see very far. I am learning from these people.'

"And the father said, 'A man who rides the horse came by the house. He was drunk and did not have much food to eat. I fed him a meal, and he told me a terribly big war has broken out in our land.' The father told the boy, 'You must choose either to wear the gray cloth or the blue cloth. I only have one leg, the other is made of wood. I can not ride a horse anymore, but you must go.'

"The son looked, and he thought and looked and thought some more. He said, 'Father, I have a third cloth to wear.' He took out a piece of white cloth and placed it between the other two pieces of cloth. 'When one side wears the gray cloth and the other side wears the blue cloth, I will wear the white cloth,' the son said. 'This is because you taught me well,' he went on. 'You sent me to the great school and I became a doctor. I know how to fix people who are sick. And also from the red ones I have learned much. I will serve my country in this way.'

"This young man became a great doctor in this war. He healed people from both sides. But in the end, this man lost everything. He lost his father's farm, lost his father, and he even lost the woman he was to marry. In the end, he had nothing. There was great bitterness toward him, and he was no longer welcome because he had not chosen the gray or blue side.

"There came a time when this young man had to leave. He left and went to a faraway land. He was trying to look for himself. This young man came to Africa and he tried to make a fortune, but he was not a man of money. He was a man who led people. Like all people whose minds are set on healing, he could keep no wealth. He found diamonds but was robbed of his discoveries. He found gold, yet everyone took it.

"In the end, he walked into the desert very far away, and there he met the people, the Bushmen. He became a healer with the people. His life ended there in the desert, where he had found his home. Because he had come by ship, people called him the Dutch word for ship.

"That young man was you. You see sir, death is not death. Death is a door that opens to another door that opens to another door. You are walking the steps you have walked before. There are twenty-one levels on this world, then you go to other worlds and then you come back to this world again.

"The white man in the story is the man who is loved by the Bushman's ancestors. He was a white man who came from faraway. He lived with the Bushmen and he died amidst them. I must tell you this: you must know and understand that death is not death, but one of the links from one life to another. This is truth. This is fact. There is no death. There is not death. When death comes, the soul must not be frightened. The mind must not be frightened."

Credo then told me of the times he had been pronounced clinically dead, including when he was stoned by an angry mob in Soweto. In these deaths he saw the same tunnel I had seen in my vision of my grandfather and with the star in the Kalahari. He also saw the place of great light that was similar to my vision when the Great Spirit showed me its face.

I told Credo I existed in the center of both good and evil. He said that was the religion of the mother, the religion of relationship and inclusion. One of the final tests of a sangoma is to find out whether he or she follows the religion of the mother. Most world religions are the religion of the father, with its emphasis on division and attempts to eradicate "the other."

Credo said the meaning of the "X" I had seen in one of my dreams involved the integration of the four winds, the coming together of the four directions. It was a holy symbol for his people. Again, my dreams were revealing that one purpose of my life had to do with bringing the different spiritual practices together.

In a moment of grave seriousness, Credo said he had little time to live and that others like me must carry on the walk. He spoke of impending ecological disasters, the corruption of African governments, and the collapse of the United States Government. The prophecies of his people matched those of the first peoples found around the world. He also warned of the petty spiritual jealousies that too often organize healers and medicine people. All forms of violence were decried, and he spoke of the necessity of all people coming together in spiritual brother- and sisterhood.

For nearly an hour, Credo Mutwa proceeded to summarize his views on psychotherapy and healing. Without knowing anything about my own work, he succinctly summarized the most basic ideas I had devoted my career to teaching. He spoke of the stupidity and dangers of psychiatric nomenclature and the necessity to always cooperate with the symptom.

Naming a problem feeds its power, he said. In his culture, problems aren't even discussed. This would empower them and make them more difficult to alleviate.

In a paradigmatic story, he illustrated how he rids a place of a "problem ghost." Rather than curse or attack the ghost or furiously demand that it leave, he establishes a respectful relationship with it and then asks how he might help it. He then helps the ghost solve its problem in a way that allows it to stop irritating the people complaining about it.

Credo argued against using the word, "AIDS." Simply saying this word was enough to hex many people into completely surrendering their lives. He believed there is a cure for AIDS involving a sonic treatment. Once, when he was a young man, he visited a tribe in central Africa that cured people with a whistle. Inaudible to the human ear, blowing this whistle near a person caused viruses to die. The people suffered no colds or influenza.

He also said a "sonic cannon" had been invented during World War II in Europe. Although built and tested, it was never used in the war. What was fascinating is that all the scientists involved in testing the sonic cannon never got a cold or viral infection. Credo said the invention is registered in a patent office and remains to be rediscovered to help fight the new killer viruses.

After talking with Credo for nearly four hours, I offered to touch him again. This time I gave him every drop of energy I was capable of passing on. My forehead touched his forehead while my body shook us together. Gentle, loving songs came forth while my hands vibrated the back of his head. The work progressed throughout his body, emphasizing the chest, legs, arms, and hands. To his right leg, filled with melanoma, I brought forth powerful spirits that aimed right at the disease. I sang into his sick lungs, placing my mouth on his troubled areas. Strong energy was sent through his hands, particularly his left hand. Near the end, my whole body held his and shook violently. Finally, I held his head, sent him highly charged love that thanked him for his life, kissed his head, and left hand and then collapsed to the floor.

What happened next was one of the most powerful spiritual experiences I have ever had with another human being. Credo changed his sitting posture and transformed into what looked like a Tibetan monk. I sat up, raised my shaking arms and hands, and began wildly chanting. Our eyes locked and we began to fuse. His spirits came forth and began directing his face to move in slow, but absolutely distinct patterns. Tilting his face to one direction, my whole body would follow and respond with a change of spirit manifestation.

Sometimes his eyes would completely roll back, exposing only the white part of his eyeballs. During all of this ceremony, Derek saw waves of light coming out of me. Derek also began to be possessed and grabbed me, chanting together with me. He was being drawn into the sangoma's reality. It was clear he would walk this path. In the minutes that followed, I completely fused with Credo and felt indistinguishable from him and one with him. It was unlike any encounter I had ever experienced or even dreamed about. Clapping wildly and shouting with ecstatic delight, I passed through another spiritual door.

Credo brought the occasion to a close by singing two spirit songs and saying these words, "This has been a very holy moment. My spirits salute your spirits. They have heard your message. Thank you very much for the sacred gift. I will now give you your sangoma spirit name. It is 'Ingwe,' the Zulu word for leopard, meaning 'the most honorable one.'" Later, viewing a photograph of Credo taken thirty years earlier, I saw that he was wearing a leopard skin looking exactly like the one I had received. He, too, was the leopard.

Without any discussion or clues, he identified me as associated with the leopard. In other encounters with sangomas, I had entered possession and been on the floor with all fours as a leopard. Furthermore, the leopard skin had recently come to me. Credo recognized the leopard, repeated the entire conversation I had had with Derek about the main points of the book I was writing, articulated my life story from the perspective of a story from another lifetime, and articulated the philosophy of therapeutic practice I had spent my entire career practicing, teaching, and writing about. He told me there was no choice but to move forward as a healer, shaman, medicine man, and sangoma. The survival of the earth required it, he argued. And lastly, the essence of Credo had fused with mine. We had become one. I felt the rest of my life somehow would be a recycling of his life story.

When we left, the sangomas and community clapped their hands with respect, and we clapped back with appreciation of their contribution and place in the spiritual world. Derek and I then proceeded to drive our car in circles in the absolute black night of back roads in the darkest of all continents. We entered a restricted mine where there was a Bushman rock painting of a leopard. Unable to see the stone, I saw and felt the leopard with my spiritual body. We had come to pay our respect to its spirit.

"X"

The very next morning a friend of Stan's came by the house to tell me she had had a dream that moved her to come over immediately. She said the night before I went to see Credo, she dreamed she was in a long tunnel with presences all around her. As she walked toward the end, voices began crying out that I had died. I knew then I had come to Africa to die and that my past was no longer my present. I had been fully reborn into being a healer with my roots going back to the Kalahari Bushmen. At the same time, my death and rebirth brought me back to where I had begun. I saw my life work as confirmed and even more important than it had seemed before. It was clear I was to walk in two parallel worlds, each feeding the other. On the one side was the world of mystery and shamanism, while the other side was the orientation of therapy I was developing based on eco-logical and systemic understandings.

Before returning to the United States, I flew to Cape Town to track down some old out-of-print books and visit the Bleek Collection at the Jagger Library, University of Cape Town. At the turn of the century, Bleek and his family transcribed approximately 12,000 pages of conversations with Bush-men. It is one of the most valuable collections of information about Bush-man life in the world. My host in Cape Town and I visited several rare book stores, museums, and galleries, discovering one obscure monograph after another related to Bushman spiritual practice. In one reprint of a lecture delivered by David Lewis-Williams, it was pointed out that the closest Bushman word for healing trance was "death." While in the Kalahari, I kept having a repeating vision of a ceremony where part of one's finger was cut off. In the Bleek papers I found a description of this very ritual performed by the Bushmen.

One of the more startling moments took place in the rare book shop, Cranford's, where the owner, Irving Freeman, told me of his interest in the Bushmen. Out of the blue I asked him if he ever heard a legend involving a white man coming to Africa after the Civil War and living the rest of his life in the Kalahari with the Bushmen. To my great surprise he had come across this story. An American did go to Africa in the late 1800's. He started in Cape Town and ended in the Kalahari where he discovered the lost city of the Kalahari. In a rare book I found a photograph of the spot marking the lost city. It was the white "X" on the ground I had seen in my dream and had asked Credo Mutwa about.

Mystery of the Bride Chamber

Upon returning from Capetown, I met Derek's wife, Sanet. What took place in their home was a remarkably startling and beautiful experience. Sanet, an artist, told me some of her previous dreams that called her to be in the spirit world. We then touched one another and instantly both of us went into a deep trance. Our hands and arms danced perfectly performed patterns of Asian-like choreographies. An oriental spirit spoke through each of us, and we gently touched various points on each other's body. Derek said it looked like we were each being used for some sort of "spirit transference."

Sanet and I were dizzy from the experience and confused as to what had taken place. I had never been in that experiential space before. It was extremely calm and smooth in its action. All body movements seemed as natural as reeds bending with the breeze.

I found it difficult to sleep that evening, trying to understand what had happened. The spirits then showed me the image of Sister Elize. When I looked at her and thought about her monastic practice, I realized the spirit looked like Marian, my companion, who also cultivated a quiet, contemplative spiritual practice. While I was in Africa, she found a tiny sea shell on a Florida beach that had a naturally carved engraving on it looking exactly like the figure of the Bushman stone drawing of a spiritual secretary bird. The spirits continued to make it clear we were to be partners.

My connection to Sister Elize may be associated with the "mystery of the bride chamber." Stephan Hoeller (*Jung and the Lost Gospels*, Wheaton, Illinois: Quest Docks, 1989, p.207) describes "the supreme mystery of the bride chamber" or "the spiritual marriage" as "the marriage of the human spirit to an angel for the Redeemer who resides in the heaven world above this earth." In the Gnostic book, *The Gospel of Phillip*, this is described as follows (cited in Hoeller, p.207):

> Everyone who becomes an offspring of the bride-chamber will receive the light. . . when he departs from the world he has already received the truth. . . . But the bride-chamber is concealed. It is the holy of holies. . . .There is a glory that is superior to glory, there is a power which is above power. Thus the perfect things are revealed to us, and so are the hidden things of the truth; and the holy things of the holy are disclosed, the bride-chamber calls unto us to enter.

In terms of uniting the feminine and masculine, the text continues:

> At the time when Eve was in Adam, then there was no death; but when she was separated from him death came to exist. If completion shall occur again, and earlier identity is attained, then death will be no more.

> If the feminine had not separated from the masculine, she would not die with the masculine. This separation became the origin of death. It was because of this that Christ came, so that he might take away the separation which was there from the beginning and thus again reunite the two; and so that he might give life to those who died while separated and make them one.

Hoeller proposes (p.209) "the transcendental bride chamber thus is said to have united God the Father with God the Mother (the holy spirit), and Jesus has replicated this divine example for the benefit of divided humanity."

In Africa, I had the experience of becoming one with two elders. Mama Mona, a seventy-two year old woman healer, gave me the spirit guides of Africa. Following my visit to her, the left side of my neck was so sore I couldn't turn it to the left. Weeks later, I met Credo Mutwa, a seventy-two-year old sangoma man, and in a deeply moving ceremony I felt one with him. Following that encounter the opposite side of my neck, the right side, was so sore I couldn't turn it to the right.

After the trip, I wondered whether Mama Mona and Credo had given me both the masculine and feminine embodiments of healing. Each was very ill and in the autumn years of a life devoted to healing. Along the path, I have been spiritually wed as one with various brothers and sisters. Most importantly, becoming a partner with Marian enabled a oneness that taps into the same spiritual source even when we are in different corners of the world.

I believe there are many people in the world who are our spiritual counterparts. When we find them and spiritually open ourselves, a spiritual bridal chamber is created. These unions are spiritual unions. Becoming one with another in this way is a loss of self and involves no sense of consuming the other. In this union the ecology of our spirituality expands into a more interconnected relational network. In this way we continue to lose our selves and become more one with the whole that encompasses us.

The Call to Die and Live

My life continues moving forward with each dream and journey. Time and time again, I learn to die and learn to live through the surrender of my life to the shamanic journey. Again and again, the call is the same. We must daily commit ourselves to creating a world where all people can pray together in music, dance, words, work, and quiet.

Toward the end of my visit with Credo Mutwa, he spoke these words to me:

"You are carrying a message. You must be brave. Throughout centuries people have been trying to stop the religion of the mother. The religion of the father separates man from nature, man from god, man from the sun, man from the stars, and man from the moon. This separation gives man free rule to do the most atrocious things upon this planet in the name of doing good. The religion of god the mother is now coming forth. The big countries are breaking up. It started with the British Empire, then the Portuguese, then the French, up until now with the Soviet Union, and soon the United States.

"The earth itself is fighting against these empires. Only when people live in small villages can they care for one another. When they care for one another, they can care for animals, they can care for the land. When we are forced to live in large communities, this caring breaks down and we risk the survival of everything. We must go back to having an existence that has a human face, a place where human beings care.

"We are being brought back to a more caring frame of mind. We must begin now to make our lives richer. We must begin now to make our lives more open. We must know that heaven is here. What we create now is what we inherit later. In healing, your battles will be long, but it will be worthwhile in the end. The human mind is evolving and changing. The problems of the mind today are not the problems of yesterday. The human mind is like the clouds in the sky, it is twisting, growing, breaking up, and coming together again. There are things today we accept that were once unacceptable.

"We are not to forget that sound has power. As healers we make sounds that (linguistically) are meaningless but have great power. When a doctor says a person has cancer, the sound of the word almost immediately makes the person give up and die. The words "cancer" and "AIDS" have a horrifying sound to people. These words must change. These names are more powerful for people than they need to be.

"Several years ago a doctor told me my leg should be cut off because of a cancer named melanoma. That name made me laugh because it sounded like the name of a beautiful girl. I asked my doctor if I was going to be killed by a beautiful girl. I told the doctor that this beautiful girl named Melanoma is not going to kill me. What I did was sculpt a gigantic statue, fifteen feet high, of this beautiful woman. I worked on this night and day and was obsessed with it. I was so weak my friends had to tie me onto ropes to make it. I completely threw myself into this project and to the surprise of my doctor, the malignant lesions disappeared.

"Whenever I feel the touch of this disease, I begin to build. In losing myself in these statues, I imagine myself beating these creatures and defeating them. Time and time again I continue to live. Every two or three years I fight this battle. In Africa the name for cancer is, Mdlazubada, the one who bites and devours you. But we never refer to it by speaking this name. We refer to it as Isahalbi, the visitor. We believe that cancer is not a disease, but a living creature.

"Every one of us exists in two worlds at once. There is another earth existing side by side with this earth. In the other earth, we are all cannibals. When a person develops cancer, we believe it involves the cannibal counterpart of ourself from the other world that is slipping into this world to devour us. When a person is attacked by cancer, he must never show fear or else he makes himself weak. Disease, being a living animal, is ahead when you are afraid. In the religion of the Great Mother, you must not call anything or anyone an enemy. If you do this, you make it stronger. We don't call the tribes we've been fighting for many years our enemy. We call them simply "the other fellows" so that they never become stronger than we are. When you have cancer, you must never panic. You must fight your sickness with a great calm. You must, above all, realize that what kills you is not so much the actual disease itself as it is your own mind that is tempted to surrender to the disease. Take your mind and occupy it fully in a very exciting project or occupation. This will give the body time to heal itself. This I know. I have kept diabetes, tuberculosis, and cancer at bay with this understanding.

"What we need now is the understanding that people are in a new stage of evolution and new diseases are coming to plague this planet. The great purification predicted by the red people and the great seers of Africa is coming, where the world will be cleansed by floods and upheavals of the weather. This time is not far away.

"Now people like yourself are sprouting like flowers all over the world. Whenever the human race goes into a major crisis, people like you appear. The American Civil War gave birth to people like yourself who started great religions. Other wars also gave birth to great spiritual ways. And now is coming another series of conflicts. Now it is not ideologies, but disease. The great hospitals will collapse under the weight of these epidemics and the doctors will run away. Some doctors have already left. They are afraid of being contaminated by AIDS.

"Who will be left holding the gap? It will be people like you. I belong to the shadow. My time is done. I can no longer help. It is up to people like you. People have forgotten how to care. We must get rid of the aggressive hero. There is nothing to avenge. We must learn to care as mother-worshipping people. We must not forget the African tribes who worshipped the goddess named Kalahari, the great fallen goddess. Kalahari means the land of the fallen woman, the fallen goddess. The "X" on the ground you dreamed about is the meeting of the four, the coming together of the four winds. The four refers to the four tornadoes that must come together in the center. At the end of the world, the great gods will have their dance. The four brothers, one must come from the west, one must come from the north, one must come from the east, and one must come from the south, will dance in the center of this X or cross. This you have seen in your dreams.

"There is something that is coming to eat the earth. I was shown this thing. I am deeply worried that a great danger is coming. According to African legend, this has happened before. There was a time when a terrible red star appeared in the sky and devoured many regions. The sea escaped from the beach and crawled all over the land. That time we feel has come.

Radio telescopes around the world are becoming inoperative. Why? I feel we are heading into a very critical time. We must join hands with each other and prepare. New kinds of tools need to be developed and new ways of healing people must be created. If the hospitals collapse and the doctors are afraid to touch people, who will be there?"

As I contemplated Credo's words, it seemed to me that a new breed of healer will be required for the troubles and plagues that increasingly confront us. These healers will be disconnected from the medieval cruelties of psychiatry and medical-minded psychologists with their lobotomizations of the connections between mind, body, and spirit. Armed with the understandings of ecology and relationship, these systemic-minded healers will utilize (rather than attack) people's symptoms and problems and help them move forward with their lives without psychiatric testing, assessment, diagnosis, medication, hospitalization, and economic ruin.

In the world of killer plagues, these healers will teach people how to die. They will show how death is a door to life. Only in learning how to die can people learn to live. To accept death is to walk the spiritual path. This same path is the only route toward life and the survival of our whole ecosystem.

AIDS may not have come to extinguish the human race, but to help save it. If it helps teach us how to die through turning us toward spirituality, it is a blessing. Of this we can be certain: the future, if there is to be one, can only be realized if we become spiritual. Conquering nature through consuming, curing and taming it, has been the very process of our own destruction. Accepting our humble part in nature through cooperating with other living creatures and accepting the mysteries of the wild will be our only healing.

The new breed of healer will reject the seductions and lies of convenient recipes and schools of therapy cooked up by modernist hucksters. They will submit themselves to the wisdom of the old ways. Spirituality, rather than economics and professionalism, will organize their practice. Stewardship, service, and sacrifice rather than exploitive profit, pseudoethical guidelines, and self-serving trade guilds will characterize their contributions. These new healers will not be professionals. They will be human beings.

The forthcoming age of healing will de-emphasize curing and accentuate healing, the making whole of one's place in the universe. In this new healing age of wholeness, all the directions will intersect. The bringing together of different spiritual traditions can wait no longer. In the sacred center point, the cross and the dance become inseparable. Here one is healed to move and moved to heal, becoming nothing and everything. Here one finds the fire of shaken spirits.

The Continuing Journey

Before returning home from Africa in June, 1992, I was awakened at three in the morning by what sounded like an explosion blowing up the front door. Without thinking, I jumped out of bed, quickly made up the bed sheets and cover to give the appearance that no one had been sleeping in the room, and dove underneath the bed. As I lay naked under the bed, three armed terrorists entered the room. I knew I would be brutally murdered if found and prayed my breathing and trembling would not be heard. I watched in absolute stillness as the light from their flashlight traced the floor around the edge of the bed. After several minutes, their noise awakened my colleague, Peter, who was sleeping in the other end of the house. A shoot out took place between Peter and the intruders, though luckily no one was seriously injured. Again, Africa had taken me to the fulcrum that tilts between life and death. After Africa, I would never be able to forget the sacred center point that holds our life.

Several weeks following my return from Africa, I received a call from an Ojibway medicine man. He said I had to leave the first thing in the morning and drive seven hours to an Indian reservation near the Canadian border. About a dozen medicine men wanted to hear what the spirits had to say. I packed and left the next morning. When I arrived, stories about visions, spirits, and the secret world of their medicine society were freely shared.

A blind medicine man eventually arrived and it was obvious that he was going to conduct a shaking wigwam ceremony. I was told not to write about the details of what took place, an event described by the medicine men as the holiest and most powerful ceremony of the Midéwiwin medicine society.

I can say that my encounter with the spirits through the mediating medicine man in the shaking wigwam dealt strictly with tasks I was to fulfill. The blind medicine man who conducted the sacred ceremony came to me and said one of the reasons it was taking place was that he saw me in a dream. In his dream I was in a desert in Africa where I joined with the spirit of a star through a tunnel. His dream was clearly connected to my experience.

In all shaking wigwam ceremonies, the individual is able to ask the spirits directly any question they desire. In my encounter, the spirits told me to find the pipe in Guadalupe, saying that when I found it, further instructions would be given. I also received the name of the place and person who would give me the otter bag I dreamed of in Africa. And finally, I was told I would enter the shaking wigwam. I am forbidden to discuss anything else about the ceremony.

Meanwhile my friends in Africa kept in touch on an almost weekly basis by phone and correspondence. Derek continued seeing Credo Mutwa regularly. Credo's health improved and he was walking again within a month and a half following our visit.

Just prior to visiting South America on July 24, 1992, I was called to meet and visit the couple in Louisiana who owned Black Elk's medicine rattle. Late on a Friday night while I was visiting their home, they brought out the rattle. I immediately felt my head experience the kind of pressure one feels when a plane drops too fast in the sky. At the same time a strong pressure hit my gut that almost made me vomit.

I immediately ran out of the house to gather my senses. Never had I felt so overpowered by an object in my life. Outside in the woods under a starry sky, something overtook me and I re-entered the house, telling the couple they could come outside if they wanted. When they came outside, I performed a ceremony with both of them. Chants and shaking took place, while I visualized the spirit of the rattle in my hand. I saw the same rattle, but it was in the form of white light and it was held over their heads.

The ceremony lasted about thirty minutes, and the couple embraced and wept deeply. I went inside the house to be alone with the rattle. The spirits put my hand on the rattle and I felt it literally burn into my right palm.

I shook it and kissed it, knowing it would always be with me. I then fully recognized that Black Elk had been the spirit guide who years ago came and instructed me about the pipe.

When the couple returned, they gave me two pieces of the rattle. They placed a piece of the thread holding the entire rattle together and a leather strip from its handle in a red cloth bundle, tied with blue string. This holy gift became the center of my altar, a link to one of the holiest human beings ever to have walked the earth.

The impact of that experience drew me to seek special prayers. The very next morning, Gary Holy Bull called, saying he had the feeling I was coming to see him. That was enough confirmation to take off to South Dakota.

As I drove toward South Dakota, I couldn't help but reflect on the early Bushman legends about the "first people" of the Kalahari. These "first people," whom the Bushmen call the "red ones" or "red people," had a very spiritually advanced culture. No one knew how their civilization had disappeared. I wondered whether the "lost city of the Kalahari" would provide us with clues for how to survive these dark times.

We know these "first people" today through ancient rock engravings. To them, the most sacred part of the evening sky was the southern cross. Underneath this sacred canopy, people learned to die and become reborn through holy weddings uniting the opposites of light and dark. In this union the holy child would be born again and again, promising new light for the future.

The spirit of light is carried in holy fires. One who transforms the spirit of fire is one who stands before the Holy Grail. African blacksmiths or sword-makers are initiated in the most secret ritual in Africa where they learn to transform the light of fire. Shamans throughout the world see this light, follow it, become married to it, and become reborn as the light. As long as these old ways continue, the light will remain. In this light are the flickers of hope for all living creatures.

When I arrived in South Dakota, Gary held a Yuwipi ceremony. Seeing the blue and white spirit lights flying through the room reconfirmed for me the part that traditional healers play in the future of all people. Healers carry the fire, the same light that ignites the dark into a blazing canopy of stars. While sitting in the sacred Yuwipi ceremony, there was a moment when I was stunned by the realization that a spirit being was actually holding each of my hands. A firm, but comforting grip was held over the middle part of each of them. In that moment I realized that the spirits both shake and calmly hold our lives in the grips of their hands.

Author with Panta Leon Rios and Senator Armando De Nucci, Argentina

I soon departed for South America and was taken to the mountains of Northwest Argentina by Senator Armando M. Perez De Nucci. Senator De Nucci is an Argentinian senator from Tucuman, a physician, and faculty member of the Tucuman Medical School. Over the years he has worked with many traditional healers in the mountains outside of Tucuman and has written several books on them. He took me to meet Panta Leon Rios, a man described as "the most powerful healer." When we met, he said I was like him. He, too, had a great vision when he was a young man. He had looked into a plate and seen the Holy Mother with smoke all around her. He knew it was a call to be a healer and soon afterwards he found he could heal animals, particularly horses. His power became so strong he could even heal horses at a distance.

When I met him, he told me he was healing people by merely looking at them. All the other healers in the mountains respected him and came to him for help and instruction. A young looking seventy-four-year-old man, he and the villagers typically live to be older than a hundred years. In a mountain area that includes puma (lion), jaguar, and magnificent winged-ones, he and his people live very close to the land.

In a ceremony, he placed his right hand into my right hand and gave me his powers. He said he was available to me at anytime and anywhere in the world. I simply had to call out for him. We looked deeply into each others eyes, touched, and allowed the spirits to shake. I also discovered that his people use the morning glory as a sacrament for a holy ceremony, the same flower I had long ago received in a dream.

In traveling around the world and meeting elders who live in the ancient ways, my own life has become reborn and remade over and over again. I now feel that I belong to the very old and the very simple. The journey seems to have no end.

As the end of my odyssey of *becoming* a healer was taking place, a new beginning of *being* a healer began to take formation. My teachers more and more came from the four-leggeds, wingeds, greens, and other non-two-legged presences. Sometimes these encounters took place in visions and other times they came from the very heart of the wilderness.

For instance, while in South America in late August, 1992, Marian and I visited a subtropical forest on the border of Brazil and Argentina. Wanting to have contact with the four-leggeds, I sang out a spiritual song. Within five seconds, animals looking like long-nosed racoons (coati) began coming out of the forest. Within several minutes dozens of these creatures had made a circle around us. They desired nothing and they searched for nothing. They simply came and were present with us. When I stopped singing, they returned to the forest.

Later that same day, we stood in front of a great waterfall. While being led by the voice of falling water, a tropical butterfly landed on our hands, one leg on Marian's hand and another on mine. The butterfly was the connective tissue bridging all three of us as one.

When I returned from South America, an opportunity arose to visit Ron Geyshick, an Ojibway medicine man living in Canada in the village of Lac La Croix. This Indian reserve has no roads or highways approaching it, so I had to fly by seaplane. Because of its isolation in the wilderness, the community has largely escaped being "contaminated" by government and church missionaries over the years. The old ways have survived and Ron is one of their holy men.

One of the men who took me there is named Charlie. I had previously met him at a shaking wigwam ceremony conducted by Dave, a blind Micmac medicine man from Nova Scotia. Charlie is highly respected by his people and regarded as a protector and custodian of Indian ways. He is often called upon to set up what is needed for sacred ceremonies. Charlie and I traveled to Ron Geyshick's home in the wilderness.

We each had an opportunity to speak alone with Ron and a shaking wigwam ceremony was held shortly after the sun went down. I cannot speak of any of the details regarding what took place in this holy event.

Ron Geyshick, Ojibway traditional teacher, with his daughter in Lac La Croix

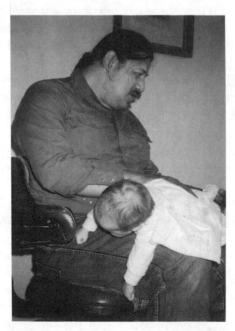

Dave Gehue, Micmac holy man, with Gage Dillabough in Nova Scotia

What I can say is that Ron said that Jesus had come and told him that He was in my heart in the same way that He was in Ron's heart. Jesus said that we each had been taught that there were no different colors of people in the spiritual world and that there are many ways to knowing the Great Creator. Jesus and other spirits, including the most holy eagle, recognized me as a healer and told Ron some specific things for me to obtain. I am permitted to say that the otter skin was found in the woods of this area. It was to become the sacred bag holding the pipe that soon would be given to me, the "pipe in Guadalupe."

After this talk, we were told to go outside and look at the sky. Flying overhead was an eagle, clearly visible in the evening sky. What was astonishing is what was above the eagle — a perfect thunderbird formed by the Northern lights. The sight was so holy that no one spoke a word. I knew I was coming close to the end of this particular journey (and the beginning of another).

Two days later I met Charlie's wife, Connie. She had called Ron Geyshick and set up our meeting. I mentioned something I was puzzled about. The night before I flew to Canada, the spirits came to me as an inner voice and said, "stop what you are doing and immediately turn on your television to channel twenty-nine. Do it now." I ran to turn on the television and instantly heard a report on mysterious white balls of light that sometimes appear in the sky. Lightning was associated with them and the balls of light often interpenetrate as if participating in some kind of mating dance. Physicists from Japan and other parts of the world could not explain what these lights were.

I told Connie and Charlie that the lights must have something to do with this trip, yet nothing about them came up at Ron Geyshick's place. They then told me they had seen those lights before. The first time they met Albert Lightning, a holy man in Alberta, those lights came out of the earth and sky.

A tremor immediately shot through my body and I gave a shout. Albert Lightning was the man who had had a vision similar to my own regarding traveling into the heavenly skies. I had spoken to Rick Lightning, his son, and Diane Meili, who wrote about him. He was a missing piece in the mystery of this story.

They said they had known Albert and that their medicine man friend from Nova Scotia, Dave, had trained and lived with him for many years. It was Dave who had previously helped me find the otter bag and pipe and had told me I would be taken inside the shaking wigwam. Charlie then showed me a pipe blessed by Albert Lighting. Albert had said the pipe was exactly like the one his father used. When I was shown this pipe, I heard a high-pitched buzzing sound. When I told this to Connie, she said that Albert had told them that the pipe had a voice and could speak to them. Once Connie was alone in a van with the pipe and heard the sound of what she thought was a bee. When she told this to Dave, he said that that was the sound of the pipe's voice.

As we talked more and more, the presence of Albert Lightning came into the room. My body began to shake and bolt. Charlie and Connie immediately said, "Albert also used to shake like that." As I was unable to hold back anymore, the spirits overtook me and we all opened ourselves to a ceremony.

At this point I asked them when Albert Lightning had died. They said that he had died when he was one hundred years old. Prior to his passing over, he told his relatives that he needed to complete one more journey before he could depart. He said he had to travel to each of the four directions and encounter the different spiritual practices. His trips took him to South America and to places in the other directions. On this journey, he was learning how to bring the different spiritual ways together to make a prayer. When this journey was complete, he went home to die.

It felt like a miracle that Albert Lightning's last vision was the same vision I had at nearly the same time. My shamanic walk as a healer began around the same time that Albert's walk ended.

Connie and Charlie left me with another story about Albert. It was about one of the last times they were with him. Albert stood in an open space and sang a holy song. Immediately many birds came to him making a circle. Everyone who witnessed this was humbled by his relationship with all living things. I wept when I heard this story and recalled how the animals had come to Marian and me when I sang to them in South America. Without a doubt, I knew that in some unexplainable way Albert and I were connected.

Perhaps I won't be permitted to write about much of my future shamanic journeying. As the walk continues, silence may be required. I do not know and I do not care. It is in the hands of the spirits.

Of this I am sure: no person is more important than any other person. We are all the same in our ignorance and in the availability of opportunities to die the death of our self-importance. Through this door, the path to spiritual truth and being is open to all. This way of fully being in life embraces respect, humility, love, and mystery. It is the most ancient of the old ways. Our hope for the future partly rests in the fact that brothers and sisters are free to say yes to the religion of the Great Mother and begin bringing our differences together in an ever changing dance. In these holy moments we may become shaken and healed together.

Mrs. Osumi

Following my visit to Canada, I received a call from Dave, the blind Micmac medicine man. He wanted to tell me many things about Albert Lightning's visions and ways of healing. Our conversation took place on October 19, 1992, a week before I was to visit Japan. This trip would mark the end of my being introduced to all the four directions of spirituality. I wondered whether this visit to the last direction would initiate uniting the different spiritual practices as one.

When I was first invited to give a speech in Japan, a book fell into my hands about the life of the great Japanese shamanic healer, Ikuko Osumi. When I found out about her, I immediately contacted the people who had invited me to Japan, asking their help in finding Mrs. Osumi. They were uable to locate her. I then asked if they could find Professor Takeshi Hashimoto, a professor of Anatomy at Toho University Medical School who had written the foreword to Mrs. Osumi's book. A few months later, just a week before I was to take off to Japan, I received a fax saying that Mrs. Osumi had been found. She lived practically right across the street from where I would be giving my speech. An appointment was scheduled for us to meet.

On the flight to Japan, an elder Asian man introduced himself and spontaneously suggested I should go to central China and learn to become a Chinese doctor. In our conversation, I found he was traveling to China to teach acupuncture. He was a master teacher of Chinese medicine and said he could immediately tell I was a natural for doing this practice. He placed his hand in front of my belly and my solar plexus began vibrating. He then placed his hands in front of my head. He had taught physicians in the United States but found they typically only used their "heads" to learn. Although they memorized all the correct information, their bodies did not have the learning to understand how to utilize *chi*, the Chinese

Mrs. Ikuko Osumi

name for the vital force. Meeting this man on my way to Japan was an omen for what was to come.

When I met Mrs. Osumi, I felt I had met the quintessential mother. She does not look exotic and probably no one would guess she is one of the greatest living healers. She is a very traditional Japanese woman whose manner exudes traditional grace and respect. Although she looked to be in her early sixties, Mrs. Osumi was seventy-four years old.

She does not speak English and when she first looked at me, she instantly began telling my translator and colleague, Professor Kenji Kameguchi, about my life. We were received in her traditional Japanese home and Professor Kameguchi privately commented that Mrs. Osumi and her household live the ways of old Japan. She served a traditional Japanese dinner and proceeded to tell me that I had learned many things from healers around the world. She commented that all these various experiences and learnings immediately needed to be made one, to be brought together as a unity.

Without telling her my full story, she knew I was on a journey to bring together the different spiritual practices. She went on to say she wanted to give me Seiki and that this would turn my many learnings into one understanding. She explained how she has a healing practice and has cured many patients over the years, treating every possible kind of disease and condition. The old and powerful families of Japan, as well as distinguished artists, religious leaders, and politicians from all over the world had been her clients.

In addition to her healing practice, she is one of only two people alive in the world who, as a Seiki master, could directly fill another person with Seiki. She carefully chooses who is to receive Seiki and typically takes a year to prepare them for receiving it. When we met, she said she must give me Seiki and that if I couldn't extend my trip for another week, she would have to travel to my home in the United States to give it to me. The only other Seiki master alive was Takafumi Okagima, her assistant, who fully agreed that I was to receive Seiki. I changed my travel plans and stayed so that she and Okagima could give me the holy gift of Seiki.

She invited me to live with her as a guest in her home and served traditional Japanese meals and tea. Throughout the week she mothered and prepared me for receiving Seiki. One evening she introduced me to Professor Burton Foreman, a university teacher of English at a Japanese women's college. He had lived in Japan and had known Mrs. Osumi for thirty-five years. Years ago he experienced a physical problem and was introduced to Mrs. Osumi. Professor Foreman provides his own account of being healed by Mrs. Osumi and of receiving Seiki (Ikuko Osumi, *The Art of Seiki*, unpublished manuscript, pp.189-197.):

> I have lived in Japan for thirty-five years. I teach English in a university in Tokyo. I have had a varied career as a teacher. I am a sports fan and I like to keep myself in as good a physical condition as possible — jogging, exercising, skiing, tennis, etc. I try to get to the gym at least twice a week. Twelve years ago, I was training regularly at Tokyo's Korakuen Stadium. One of the reasons I began weight-lifting was because I have had a weak stomach for as long as I can remember and I thought weight-lifting might strengthen me somehow. Hyperacidity had kept me on antacid tablets for many years.
>
> A friend of mine, Mrs. Emiko Matsumoto, introduced me to Osumi-sensei. Emiko's husband had been operated on for cancer of the throat, but gradually his condition had worsened, despite the operation. Finally, in desperation, she turned to Osumi-sensei. In a matter of a few weeks, her husband, Masao, showed such remarkable improvement that I became curious. Emiko extolled the virtues of this Osumi-sensei to such an extent that I finally decided to give her a try.
>
> This all was happening during the period I was weight-lifting

at Korakuen Stadium. I continued my bench press activity and felt I was growing some muscle, but something else was growing, too, in my left arm and on the left side of my body . . . a pain. I put this down to hyperacidity. Hyperacidity had always produced strange results with me in that I had felt pain in the region of my heart and even in my arms. I had come to associate that with heartburn and the general discomfort of acidity. Finally I consented to visit Osumi-sensei and to receive a treatment. My left side hurt so inordinately that I gave in.

The day decided upon turned out to be one of the most painful days for me. Not only was my left side hurting, but my stomach was on fire. A maid ushered me upstairs into a six-mat tatami room. There was a Japanese bedroll laid out for me on the tatami flooring and I noted the fusuma, the typical colorful sliding doors of Japanese houses, leading to another room. The fusuma was closed. I was told to change into a yukata, a Japanese-type bathrobe, and lie down on the bedroll. My left arm ached and the pit of my stomach was on fire.

Osumi-sensei slid back the fusuma and stepped into the room. She got down on her knees beside me. She first joined the palms of her hands together, as she knelt at my right side, and briefly made a bow, as is the custom of Buddhist believers. She next picked up my right hand and felt my pulse. Emiko had told me that she always begins a treatment by feeling the pulse. According to Emiko, it is the feel of the pulse which zeroes Osumi-sensei in on the location of the patient's malady. Osumi-sensei felt my pulse for thirty seconds or so. She looked at me in a very enigmatic manner, stood up, walked completely around me, and got to her knees again at my left arm. She picked it up and began massaging the very spot which ached the most. If that wasn't surprising enough, what Osumi-sensei said quite astounded me. As she continued gently rubbing my arm, she said: "Why are you trying to hide this from me? This is where your real trouble is. What have you been carrying that is so heavy?"

I lay there stunned. She knew about the pain in my left side! Her remark was unbelievable. She had understood about weights I had been lifting, not directly, but knew that I had had considerable weight of some sort in my hands and arms. I was quite surprised, to put it mildly. Was Emiko right, after all?

I watched her with a changed attitude as she rose up on her knees and towered over my body. She raised her right hand above her head and inhaled with a startling intake of air. She sucked the air into her lungs like the slurp of a vacuum cleaner consuming a large piece of paper. She then exhaled the air in a loud noise between her teeth. Again she drew in a deep gulp of air. Then, with her lungs full, she began to lower her head in a peculiar manner. It began with a large whirl of her hand, which she rotated quickly in a vast circle in midair as though gathering force from some unseen object. She then closed the circumference of the circle as her hand approached my arm so that the entire movement resembled a vortex. She aimed the point of the vortex at my arm. She stopped her hand just over it. Her face was contorted as she still held her breath.

I can only say it was as though she had made a great effort of some sort in drawing out something — what, I don't know — from the air about her and now held it in her lungs. Then, quite suddenly, she bent down and blew the air over my arm until she completely emptied her lungs. She gently began to massage my arm while, at the same time, she inhaled and exhaled air again and again in a very rapid manner immediately above my arm, blowing air onto it as she rubbed it.

It was a weird and rather frightening experience for me, so unexpected and startling had it all been, and so uncharacteristic of the gentle woman.

A state of euphoria began to creep over me. I can't say at which moment or at which movement of this unusual woman I felt the pain leave my arm, but it disappeared, and I felt released of something unwanted and unhealthy within me.

After massaging my arm for some time, she gently laid it down and asked me to turn over on my stomach. She then began to massage my spinal column. I have learned since then that each vertebra contains the nerve to various centers of your body — the kidneys, lungs, etc. — each of which Osumi-sensei will enumerate as she works down your back.

If the back treatment is wonderful beyond description, then the climax of the head treatment is unforgettable. This is something one has to experience to understand the depth of sheer comfort her fingers produce when she begins on your head.

I started my treatments that summer sometime toward the end of July, 1975. By the end of August, I was a different person. The pain in my side had completely disappeared. I felt wonderful. I was at peace with my stomach. But now I had a new problem, and that was to understand what Osumi-sensei was talking about when she spoke of "Seiki."

I talked with Emiko about this and she said that Osumi-sensei was trying very hard to make me understand what "Seiki" was. I was the first foreigner she'd ever treated.

Osumi-sensei talked to me about Seiki at every treatment. "Seiki" means "life force," she explained. "The human body has power to cure itself. Unhealthy cells are complemented by healthy ones. While struggling to maintain a hormone balance, the body produces healthy cells which rehabilitate the nerves. The lymph glands expel the unwanted unhealthy cells. Because of a natural amount of Seiki in your body, the exhaustion accumulated over the day is expelled from the ordinary, healthy person through the power of his body. Seiki aids in the process.

We are exposed to Seiki in the atmosphere," she continued. "But, by agitating the atmosphere in the form of a vortex I have learned how to concentrate this natural force and increase its effective power. I direct this concentrated power toward the unhealthy areas of my patients." This concentration of Seiki, doubling or tripling its natural force, is what is unique about Osumi-sensei's treatments.

I learned that besides the regular treatments, Osumi-sensei can instill this power permanently from the atmosphere into the human body in an incipient form, after which the person who had Seiki instilled in him must nourish it, so to speak, by special exercises.

So it was on July 4th, 1976, in addition to the regular treatments I had been receiving for a year, I had Seiki instilled in me. Osumi-sensei told me that it takes about a year of prepatory treatments for a patient's body to be in a condition to receive Seiki in a very concentrated, permanently residing form.

What happened was a very strange and wholly unexpected experience for me. On that day I was seated on a stool in a small room. With Osumi-sensei were two assistants. They all stood behind me. I waited patiently, although apprehensively. The time had arrived for me to "receive Seiki." I felt nervous. Quite suddenly and entirely unexpectedly there arose behind me the most dreadful din I have ever heard in my life. I heard shouting, hissing and then the sound of pounding. I realized all three of them were hitting the fusuma with the open palms of their hands.

I experienced yet another shock when one of the assistants began to breathe into my right ear in an ever-increasing crescendo until he was hissing, blowing out puffs of air, and uttering meaningless bursts of sound . . . while the other two were shouting at the tops of there lungs, giving forth meaningless yells and shrieks, which produced in total the most God-awful racket one could ever imagine.

I sat there shocked. I shall never forget that moment when, quite suddenly, I felt something come down from above me . . . from the direction of the ceiling, down into my head! Something was entering my head in the back where the hair-whorl is located.

I thought: "My God! This is it!" It was like a light electric shock, yet one that moved slowly down the back of my neck and into my spinal column. I felt frightened for the first time. Whatever it was was inside me and moving down my back. I could feel it moving, not too fast, yet moving slowly down. I can say this about it. It was something with a purpose.

But then what followed was even more surprising and unexpected. I saw Osumi and her two disciples appear at my right side and stand looking at me expectantly. The moving sensation in my body reached the very bottom limits of my spinal chord — the tail bone, and I knew that that was its destination. I was then suddenly, totally unexpectedly, thrown forwards on my stool in a violent thrust surging up from my tail bone. The upward surge threw me completely off the stool.

The surprise of it staggered me. But one of the disciples shouted at me. "Get back up on the stool!" I scrambled back up, but hardly had I sat down again when, just as unexpectedly and as equally sudden as I had been thrust forwards, I was next drawn back in a swift pull from behind and jerked so far back that my legs flew up into the air directly over my head so that I was tottering on the back edge of the stool. I can remember the surprise of that so well, because I did not fall over backwards off the stool as I most certainly would have under ordinary conditions. My feet were up in the air almost directly over the stool and I should have tumbled right off backwards, but no! — something was holding me, something at my hip was preventing me from falling over backwards. In fact, this something was so powerful that before I could fully digest this very strange situation, I was again pulled forwards in a violent thrust from my hips, and again I was thrust forwards. My legs slammed down on the floor and my face all but banged into them. But — then, again I was pulled backwards. My feet were high up in the air again and I was tottering on the edge of the stool again. But I did not fall over backwards, nor even have the sensation that I might fall over backwards. I felt entirely secure in whatever had gripped me in its powerful, vice-like control.

It was then, when I was thrust forwards again and pulled backwards again for the third time, that I heard Osumi-sensei from my right shout out: "Look! The sun! It's shining!" What was she saying? Her shout was so mingled with the surprise of this violent movement which thrust me about that it took a time for the meaning to sink in.

I remember turning my head to look toward the window. The brilliance of the sun surprised me, but I was much too preoccupied with my rocking motion to consider the importance of the sun at that moment. However, what I do sense and remember as being a fundamental part of that strange morning was Osumi-sensei's delight at seeing that sun.

"Congratulations!" she cried to me, finally, "You have received Seiki. It is in you for life. Cherish it."

So it was I "received" Seiki on July 4, 1976. The noise and the heavy breathing, I learned, is to "activate" the Seiki in the atmosphere into a concentrated form. What was unusual about my particular reception of Seiki was that there were three people working together to activate Seiki. I learned later that usually only Osumi-sensei alone, or at most with one disciple, attempts to "bring down" Seiki, as she calls it. Since I was the first foreigner to "receive Seiki" from her, she had called in reinforcements, so to speak, to make sure the results were positive. Those results had even astonished her, it seems. The three of them working together had produced a triple-fold amount of Seiki surging down into my body with the resultant violence of this concentrated force.

I also learned later that when Osumi-sensei and her disciple or disciples sense that Seiki is beginning to move down from somewhere out in the atmosphere, they put their hands on top of each other, just barely touching the top of the head. This way their hands become conductors of Seiki, she told me.

After a person has 'received Seiki' there are exercises to do every day which reinforce the power of Seiki within that person who receives it. These are done on a special stool in a type of rocking motion of the body. Done just before you retire, the exercises guarantee a sound, dreamless sleep during which the body is renewed and invigorated.

This is a true experience, and I wish to state that I know that there is something within me which I still don't fully understand, but which Osumi-sensei says will be with me for life . . . prolonging and guarding my life.

When Professor Foreman and I met, he expressed his surprise that Mrs. Osumi was giving me Seiki with less than a week of preparation. He said this had never been done before. We were entertained by the fact he had been the first foreigner to receive Seiki and I was to be the first to receive it so soon after being introduced to her.

Professor Foreman added that she explained to him that I was ready for Seiki and she wanted to give it to me as a gift because she knew how many people I was going to help. She later told me that when we met, the spirit of my grandfather on my father's side and grandparents on my mother's side asked her to have me stay with her. They knew I needed to have the many different spiritual lessons transformed into one. Otherwise, the many unintegrated differences might physically wear me down. The following day her own spirit ancestors told her she was definitely to give me Seiki.

Professor Foreman said how very unusual it was for a foreigner to be so well received by a traditional Japanese household. He stated I should appreciate the unique graciousness given to me, noting that she had given me the status of a family member. In thirty-five years of living in Japan, he said he had never seen anything like this.

In the week of preparing for Seiki, I felt completely loved and nurtured by Mrs. Osumi. She carefully planned my days and watched over every

Author with Burton Foreman and Mrs. Ikuko Osumi

detail of attention given to me. The intensity and closeness of our connection is impossible to describe. We would sometimes silently gaze at one another like a mother and son who hadn't been together for years. It was one of the most touching weeks of my life.

She seemed to know everything about me in all my aspects. She knew my right eye aches and my waist weakens when I become overworked and exhausted. She knew that I was working on this book, *Shaking Out the Spirits*, and made suggestions for how it should be completed. Furthermore, she specifically told me what to do with my personal relationships.

When I called home to make arrangements for staying longer in Japan, I felt an earthquake in the room as I explained the forthcoming reception of Seiki. The next day I discovered no one else had felt the earthquake. Clearly, Seiki was making its presence known.

My time in Japan was very therapeutic. My speeches were well received and one audience member stood up and said I spoke like a Zen teacher. I was later to find he had been a friend of Alan Watts and had translated his book, *Psychotherapy East and West*, into Japanese. I became friends with many Japanese psychotherapists, and two of my former students, Edward and Yuriko, joined me on a visit to Kyoto, walking through the many holy shrines and gardens. Standing before the Golden Pavilion was like receiving a bath in all aesthetic eternity. It is one of the most beautiful spots on earth.

The famous Zen rock garden at Ryoanji Temple revealed to me that it was an instrument for helping empty one's mind. From the far corner, the entire length of the garden completely fills one's visual field extending from the limits of each side of one's peripheral vision. While filling one's eye with this whole space one may consciously note which cluster of rocks receives the most of one's attention. Noting this, one spreads one's attention to another rock cluster, and then another, until equal attention is given to all clusters. The moment this takes place, one's mind is completely full with no room for thought. At that moment the mind opens and achieves a natural state of emptiness.

Returning from Kyoto, Mrs. Osumi introduced me to patients and friends who spoke about her healing gifts. One friend was a master teacher of *bonseki*, the art of using sand and stones to create an image on a lacquer tray. She came to the house, asked me to select a drawing, and then created it on her lacquer surface. I was moved by the refinement of her movements and her ability to create a landscape and a universe in such a small space and in just a moment.

On the day before I was to receive Seiki, Mrs. Osumi and her assistant gave me several Seiki massages to prepare my body. I was told to rest all day and not to leave my room. The next morning, I would be given Seiki.

As I lay in bed that evening, I thought of all the many different encounters and experiences of my spiritual journey. How fitting it would be if the moment of making all these different spiritual experiences one would be facilitated by a great mother, a woman embodying the practice of the Great Mother. Emphasizing relationship and unity rather than difference and separation was the main characteristic of what Credo Mutwa had called "the religion of the Great Mother." In Japan I was placed in the arms and hands of such a mothering spiritual practice.

Perhaps here I would realize the prayer of unifying the different spiritual practices. Mrs. Osumi had been preparing for a month to give Seiki to someone on November 7. When we met, she knew it was for me. It is no easy task to give Seiki. The first time she gave it, all her teeth fell out. It took her time and patience to master this pre-Buddhist healing practice.

Some of her clients had seen whirl-wind-like clouds enter the room when she gave Seiki. I was sure this was the same wind known inside the shaking wigwam and in other healing ceremonies around the world. She told me that Seiki comes to her from the whole cosmos and travels around the earth, concentrating into a whirl-wind entering her special room. This room was perfectly aligned with the universe in a way that facilitated and concentrated the flow of Seiki. In the week prior to my receiving Seiki, she said the Seiki for me was moving from Ireland to Anchorage, Alaska, through the continental United States, to Hawaii and coming toward her house in Tokyo. Interestingly, she had not known of my Irish ancestors.

Her preparation for giving Seiki involves completely emptying her mind and establishing a oneness with her client. By the time November 7 came, I completely trusted and loved this woman. I knew I would surrender my mind and will to become one with her relationship with Seiki. I had a sense of wonder over how one of the words for "treatment" in Japanese is "teate" which literally means to put one's hands on another's body. All the ancient traditions of healing throughout the world acknowledged and utilized what Professor Hashimoto called the "skinship" between patient and therapist. How unfortunate this wisdom is being lost in contemporary practices of therapy with their so-called professional guidelines prohibiting any connection of skin.

I also was moved by Mrs. Osumi's own story about how she had learned from her experiences in nature. She studied all aspects of nature, carefully watching how animals cure themselves, studying the relationships between the tides and climate, and, in particular, becoming a master of caring for plants, particularly orchids. Studying how each plant requires individual attention taught her how to take care of the unique needs of each patient.

My week of preparing for Seiki had been marked by perfect fall weather, with the sun shining every day. On the evening before I was to receive Seiki, a thunderstorm broke out. This was always a strong sign for spiritual work. In the morning, the sky was cloudy and the air very still. As I was taken to the preparation room and given a massage, the wind began blowing. It blew harder and harder until every door and window in the house rattled and shook. I began to fear a typhoon was coming. Later I found out that the Tokyo meteorologists had, in fact, announced typhoon conditions at that very time. As the wind grew stronger, Mrs. Osumi and Mr. Okagima said that the Seiki was so strong they couldn't hold it any longer. Although they typically give it at around noon time, the whirling energy was so intense it had to be released mid-morning.

Moments before receiving Seiki, I had a vision of an ancient Japanese man in a traditional robe. The robe had a design of waves with fish. He held two swords crossed as an "X" with the intersecting center held in front of his solar plexus. Mrs. Osumi later said he was probably her ancestor who had come to protect me from any bad influences.

Going to the tiny room with the Seiki bench, I sat on it, was positioned, and the ritual began. It seemed so fast that I'm not completely certain about what really happened. I do remember noises being made, the wind blowing, and a ring of heat and electrical energy on the top of my head. My body jolted in the way it had when I was baptised at New Salem, and my whole being vibrated up and down in various patterns. After a while, Mrs. Osumi touched the bottom of my spine and the shaking stopped. She said, "Congratulations. You have received Seiki."

I was taken to a room to rest and reflected over how this experience was familiar to me. It was the same energy I had felt when I had the great vision at nineteen years of age. It was the same force that taught me vibratory body work. And over the last four years, I had experienced this energy at New Salem, the Kalahari, and in almost all my most holy spiritual experiences.

After about thirty minutes of resting, Mrs. Osumi and Mr. Okagima came to give me instructions for how to "nurture" Seiki daily through a series of exercises. By pressing on one's eyelids, the rocking movements are initiated. Allowing one's body to move this way as long as it desired was encouraged. They also showed me an exercise of banging my feet on the ground as a way of helping rest my head.

When they sat me down on a Seiki bench, I immediately began vibrating in a variety of patterns. They claimed they had never seen anyone go into this movement so quickly after Seiki, so they proceeded to give their follow

Seiki bench in Mrs. Osumi's home

up session. In this encounter, I asked Mrs. Osumi if I could touch her and show how I use this energy to heal. When I touched her, an enormous amount of energy came forth. It was so strong she had to help me settle it down.

She then said only two people in the world have mastered Seiki and can give it directly to others. I was to be the next Seiki master, she added. Mrs. Osumi became very excited and talked about how special the week had been and that she wanted me to return soon to spend time healing her clients. She instructed me to continue healing people in the United States, saying "touch many people with your hands." When I came back to Japan, she would teach me more through working with her clients. At the end of that time, she would present me with a Seiki bench.

That evening, Mrs. Osumi arranged a "Seiki celebration party" at the Imperial Hotel. She treated everyone with an extravagant French dinner. I then found out how fortunate I had been to have been freely given Seiki by Mrs. Osumi. She seldom gives Seiki, partly due to the enormous stress it puts on her body. She wouldn't give it again for five months. She celebrated the announcement that I would be able to give Seiki in the future. She began giving me special instructions concerning my diet, including fresh lemon and apple juice every day. We planned a project for making a video tape of her doing Seiki exercises as well as healing patients. And finally she commented on how I was to take care of my son, Scott, because she believed he was to be a very important person. She gave me gifts for him including special raw silk "soaked" with Seiki to help heal any bronchial troubles he might develop. In addition, she said she wanted to give him Seiki.

Following the dinner celebration, we returned to her home and talked more about her healing practice, the spiritual world, and my destiny as a healer. She was very clear that I was to work in two worlds — as both a university professor and a healer.

As had been set forth in her own story, (*The Art of Seiki*, see pp. 189-197) Ikuko Osumi has many shamanic powers, including the ability to see in the future. Throughout the week, she celebrated what she saw as a very successful future for me in both the healing and creative arts. She said to confidently expect this and receive it naturally. She also predicted I would get married within the year. Six months later, Marian and I were married in a ceremony blessed by the presence of a spectacular arrangement of flowers sent by Mrs. Osumi.

I left Japan feeling I had met my "Spiritual Mother." She had helped me realize that everything I needed had already been with me. As I had died and been reborn in Africa, she helped mother me through the infancy and childhood of accepting my gifts as a healer. She is always present in the deepest place of my heart.

On my return flight to the United States, I thought about two powerful dreams I had in Japan. On the night before receiving Seiki, I dreamed of how I previously had seen God as being pure light and energy. Now I was shown how this light may be transformed into any form, making it possible for all people to have an encounter with the God force. It is natural that all great spiritual leaders have been seen at times as pure light. My dream showed me how all these spiritual people and traditions are born from the same source — the raw, pure, undifferentiated light and energy called Seiki, chi, ki, num, or holy spirit, among other names. When a human being sees a form of spirit, whether it be Christ, Buddha, a spirit eagle or snake, the form is a creation brought about by the interaction of a specific tradition with the unformed energy. In this way, all traditional images, spirits, and practices are one. They all belong to the great ocean of one light.

With this dream, I found all my different experiences in diverse traditions returning to the first great vision of my life when I saw the holy light.

My journey toward integrating the different spiritual practices ended by returning me to my beginning vision. In the beginning of my walk, I was given a spiritual answer. It took many years to unfold the question enabling an understanding of that beginning answer. In this circular path, I began at the end and ended at the beginning.

Amazingly, at the very time I was staying with Mrs. Osumi, Credo Mutwa, the great Zulu sanusi, sent word that he wanted me to know something. When I returned from Japan, I was told he had been thinking about my dream of seeing an "X" on the ground with a sword next to it. His spirits told him I was now ready to pick up the sword and draw a circle in the ground around the "X." The four directions marked by the "X" were to be made one by a circle circumscribing them. His message was issued as Mrs. Osumi helped me unite the four directions and as I recognized the completion of the circular path returning me to the beginning of my spiritual walk.

Credo sent instructions for me to find a blacksmith and have him make a sword, and go conduct the ceremony he described. In a vision, I saw the sword I was to make. In its handle was a snake with an emerald in its center point and four lines going out from the stone. The next day I went to the bookstore to see if this design could be found. I quickly encountered the book, *Dreambody* by Arnold Mindell (Boston: Sigo Press, 1982, p.136-137) in which the following words sent a shiver through my body: "The sword represents the power of the shaman, hero, priest, and warrior . . . the sword is used to govern the snake world, the world of subtle energies . . . The hero who wanted his sword to work well for him had to talk to and win the friendship of the snake that inhabited the sword." The next day I found a blacksmith who helped me make the sword.

My life evolves forward every day in the nurturing of the light, Seiki, or holy spirit(s) within me. My body shakes as it needs to and in this shaking the maturity of my healing practice develops. I continue to be shown more visions and taken to holy people and places. As Mrs. Osumi, Credo Mutwa, Mama Mona, Gary Holy Bull, Ron Geyshick, and others have declared, it has become my responsibility to touch others to help awaken the vital life force within them.

The activation and nurturance of this vital breath of life connects each of us to the whole cosmos. We become fed by the life of all living things. Living this way not only makes us more respectful of other life, it gives us more life. Our bodies become more vibrant and healthy. This fountain of life is found when we receive Seiki, the vital breath of life.

The last dream I had in Japan touched me deeply. My son's dog, Sherlock, who recently had died, came to me as a spirit dog. When I tried to lift my arm and hand to touch him, something very unusual took place. Another arm and hand lifted out of my physical arm and moved to pet him. I was able to touch and feel him through this other arm. I wept as I stroked him for the last time and wondered whether I was being taught to use this other hand to touch others.

In my last conversation with Mrs. Osumi before leaving Japan, I conveyed this dream. She told me how one depiction of the Buddha has many hands and arms, enabling many sentient beings to be helped. She said I also had many hands and arms and my responsibility was to heal many people. She mentioned how she sends Seiki to people all over the world and took photographs of my family so she could protect and nourish them with her hands that reached across the ocean.

One of my last comments to her concerned my certainty that her healing came from her love as much as it did from Seiki. She smiled and agreed. We hugged each other, knowing we would always be together in spirit through spiritual hands and arms.

Receiving the Pipe and the Holy Grail

In my journey around the world, I have linked my arms with other spiritual arms. This circle of healers is the community my healing practice takes place in. My acts of healing are always joined by the spirits and the spiritual touching of the great healers of many ancient healing traditions. I am only a link that helps bring all of this touching to someone needing to be healed or awakened.

The week following my stay with Mrs. Osumi was marked by an avalanche of healing and changes around me. My colleagues claimed I had changed, looked different, and my secretary even remarked that my hand-writing had changed. While in Japan, Mrs. Osumi told me I should get married soon and that my son would also tell me this. When I returned, my son immediately told me he wanted me to get married. He also had a bronchial condition, the trouble with his lungs Mrs. Osumi had reported. I spoke with his mother, and we both agreed to do what Mrs. Osumi prescribed. When my son opened his birthday gift from Mrs. Osumi, he found a beautiful porcelain heart filled with chocolates. We keep that heart in our home, and we never forget how this great healing mother has touched our lives.

Two weeks after receiving Seiki from Mrs. Osumi, I awakened in the middle of the night and had the incredible feeling of being connected to the whole cosmos. In this sacred encounter, what Bucke once called "cos-mic consciousness," I remembered the same deep sense of calm and know-ing accompanying my first vision. While being absorbed in what was taking place, one of the most remarkable moments of my life occurred. I felt and became the breathing of the one breath that breathes the entire universe.

The very next night, the experience repeated itself. This time, however, I was startled due to my feet and legs becoming very hot. Although I had experienced heat in my upper body, never had the fire touched these parts. In these experiences, I knew all my past learnings were continuing to be made one.

With each day, the unsolved mysteries of my shamanic journey were being unravelled and brought to a unified understanding. One morning I was awakened and told by the Great Spirit to go to my spiritual altar and tepee. I was told I would find the "pipe in Guadalupe." Putting my face into the center circle of stones, I saw the Yuwipi spirit lights and suddenly knew I could fly as an eagle to the shrine of our Lady of Guadalupe. I flew there as an eagle spirit and noticed how she was standing on the horns of a bull. After remembering she was red-skinned and sent to help Indians, I was knocked over by a voice that said, "She is White Buffalo Calf Woman, the holy woman who gave the Indians their sacred pipe."

"The Pipe in Guadalupe" referred to the pipe creator, White Buffalo Calf Woman, who appeared in another time and place as our Lady of Guadalupe. At that moment, the spirits revealed to me the pipe that I was to care for. I was shown its design and told I would find someone who could make it.

When I later drew the design, I wondered if anyone would be skilled enough to make it. I also felt the heaviness of being the caretaker of a pipe given to one by White Buffalo Calf Woman. I marveled over how Our Lady of Guadalupe and White Buffalo Calf Woman were one. I later discovered they were also the same as the Holy Virgin Mother, Sister Elize, and all other sacred mothers. Each was a different manifestation of the one Great Mother. In my spiritual encounter with the great mother, Ikuko Osumi, all my different spiritual learnings returned to their source and birth place, the original life-giving Great Mother.

On the very day I was shown the pipe, I received a call from Charlie in Canada asking me if I had any pipestone. He said the Cree carver, Frank Morin, was visiting him and wanted to carve a pipe. When I told him my dream, we both knew his call was no accident.

Needing some pipestone, I called my friend, Sam, who quarries the stone at Pipestone. He was out of town, but his mother said, "Sam just placed some pipestone out in the front yard for some people who worked with him in the quarries. Since they never picked it up, you're welcome to take a piece." I was amazed at how the stone was waiting there to be picked up. The pipe from Guadalupe was found and made.

In the Pipestone National Park museum is displayed a remarkable piece of pipestone having the natural image of a pipe on it. I call this pipe image the "holy signature" for the whole territory. It marks the holy purpose of

Sam Gurnoe

The "pipe" signature stone

the site. This sacred signature in stone was found in Sam's quarry and the pipestone for my pipe lay next to it.

On the same day that my pipe was born, I received a letter from a government ranger in Khutse Reserve, Kalahari Desert, Botswana. He said the old Bushman chief came and wanted him to write me a letter. I had given the chief my address and explained he could reach me by asking someone to write. The letter said the chief wanted me to know I was their "saver." He also said his days were numbered and now was the time to tell him anything I needed to tell him.

I knew I must pass on Credo's words about dying and tell him we would be connected when he crossed over into the other side. How fitting it was that the end of my journey of initiation as a healer included contact with the man who helped me die and become reborn as a healer in the Kalahari. Now I would help him die and become reborn as a healer in the Great Desert in the Greater Sky.

Two days following the letter from the Kalahari, I went to an exhibition on the life of the Plains Indians entitled, "Visions of the People" held at the Minneapolis Institute of Arts. In the first room of the exhibition was a "visionary image" drawn in 1880 by Yellow Nose, a Northern Cheyenne Indian. The vision provided a powerful confirmation of my recent experiences. It showed a man receiving a pipe from White Buffalo Calf Woman. He was covered with seven stars, the number of stars put around my neck by Sister Elize. The star over his heart was depicted as an "x" inside a circle. Witnessing the sacred exchange was an eagle with a snake in its beak. This vision contained many of the sacred images of my shamanic journey and came to me immediately following my reception of the pipe from the Great Goddess.

The very next night I was awakened at 1:30 a.m. by the sound of a car door slamming shut. I found myself in the middle of a dream where I was in the Middle East on what appeared to be an archeological dig. My sister, who had been in a dream with Sister Elize a year ago, and I had just discovered a huge stone under the ground. Upon closer examination it was revealed as a perfectly clear crystal. I looked and saw an image etched onto it that was a convergence of all the images carved on my pipe. I stared again and in the center of the stone-crystal was a perfectly formed cross. I knew I had found the Holy Grail. In between the cross and the converged image was an "X" or cross with a circle around it. Around that circle was another circle. In this circle around the circle, I realized I was facing the completion of my shamanic initiation. The end of this particular journey was now complete.

Within months of having a sense of completion, I received a letter or phone call from practically every healer I had met from all around the world. As hard as it may be to believe, they all contacted me at approximately the same time. Every healer urgently told me to visit them.

I was overwhelmed by the impossibility of being able to travel to all four corners at the same time. Furthermore, I felt the shamanic call was becoming too much for me to handle and one evening while praying for help, the words of William Tall Bull echoed back, "Just follow what the Spirits tell you to do."

In what became a crisis of absolute despair and frustration, I knew I would not visit all the spiritual people who were calling. In this time of surrender, I decided I would not rely on any of them to guide me any more. I pledged that from that moment on I would focus my learning and guidance solely upon the One Great Spirit.

With this decision, I became flooded with the realization that I am truly nothing. I felt completely unworthy and unable to be a healer of any kind. I thought of my son and family and decided then and there that it would be enough simply to live. At that moment I sincerely gave up being a shaman and healer. It was too much to bear and I was not strong enough to make the sacrifices and carry the burden associated with it.

A voice immediately told me to take down my spiritual altar. I found a special suitcase and placed all my spiritual items in it. I was then instructed to place this in a private place and to curb discussing the spiritual visions that would come to me in the future.

When the suitcase was packed and hidden away, I said to myself, "I do not want to speak of these things again," "I only want to live."

A voice startled me by quickly responding, "You have passed the final test. There are no medicine people, shamans, or healers. There are only people who sacrifice themselves so that others may be healed. You had to sincerely give up what was given to you to fully receive it. This walk must now be done with humility."

In these shamanic journeys, I was carried around the world. The reception of spiritual gifts from all the four directions made me full, too full in fact, to carry the burden of being a shamanic healer. In this fullness I desired and was returned to nothing. I was left with the wisdom that being alive is enough.

Healing Waters

After I put away my suitcase, I began having visions of the stick and feathers I was to find among the Guarani Indians in Paraguay. As I mentioned at the beginning of this story, these South American Indians gave me protection and helped me learn how I was to carry forth with my life. At the conclusion of that journey in the rain forests, I returned to Asuncion with a strong desire to see the shop we had visited during my first day in Paraguay. We went and the sacred stick with its feathers was still there. I told the shop manager how my dreams brought me to South America. She was moved and handed me the object saying, "This is for you."

The man who had mysteriously left it there just prior to my arrival was a Chamacoco Indian shaman located near the border of Bolivia. The shamanic practice of his people reminded me of African traditions. The

creatures in his territory not only included the winged ones, but the crocodile and the leopard. Furthermore, their shamanic practice was best char-
acterized by the shaking of the shaman. Somewhere among the Chamacoco
Indians was a shaman who dreamed the same sacred object I had and
made it available for me to find. He, too, shook and was connected to the
crocodile and the leopard.

When I returned home, I made the sacred object shown in my dreams.
When it was complete, I was amazed to see the extent to which it looked
like a tree. A stick in the shape of a "Y" had six feathers on each side of
its top branches with blue thread wrapped around the end of each feather.

As I held this sacred tree, I realized that the golden-yellow color of one
side of the feathers was the light, the holy light helping give birth to life.
The blue circling the feathers was connected to the cleansing waters needed
to sustain life. With this light and water, I was reminded of how healing
may return to a dying earth. The trace of green on the backside of the
feathers suggested that such vital life can return.

A week later I was shaken by the realization that Black Elk's great vision
ended with his being given a stick to plant in the center of a sacred hoop.
This stick, given by the six spiritual grandfathers who gave him his vision,
was to be used to help bring back the tree of spiritual life, a reawakening
of the old spiritual ways and a healing of our Mother Earth — a healing
of the sacred circle.

In the latter days of his life, Black Elk climbed Harney Peak, praying and
lamenting to the six grandfathers to help the stick bloom and bring his
people back within the sacred hoop. In his vision, the Great Spirit told
Black Elk, "When you go forth to the center of the nation's hoop you shall
run to the four quarters." In my journey, I learned that finding the center
of spirituality required going to different spiritual directions and experiencing their connection to the same Great Center. I believe the sacred hoop
will be reconnected again when the different spiritual traditions are able
to come together and make a prayer to preserve their old ways as a means
of saving the earth.

In Black Elk's vision, he saw what he called a "blue man" symbolizing
those who have harmed Mother Earth. In their greed and selfishness, they
have tried to tie a knot around the end of each of the six sacred grandfathers, blocking their connection to us. This same color of blue, however,
represents the healing and cleansing waters that can bring back our connection to spiritual life. Our mission is to transform these blue knots into
healing waters enabling the spiritual tree of life to heal itself and blossom
again. If we do not transform them through practicing the old spiritual
ways, then Mother Earth herself will release the greater cleansing waters.

As I hold the tree of life my dreams gave me, I see six feathers on each of two branches. The coming together of six spiritual leaders from the north and six spiritual leaders from the south will help loosen the blue knots. This loosening will bring forth a nourishment of the old spiritual ways. This small step toward bringing these two directions together moves us closer to closing the sacred circle and making it one again.

My spiritual journey began with a vision in front of the building holding the first written record of Black Elk's great vision. It came to a full circle when I stared at a sacred stick revealing a tree of spiritual life. At that time, I studied Black Elk's vision and found my vision encircled by his. Our different journeys became the same in that moment of facing the sacred tree in the sacred hoop.

Each of us must find his/her own vision and follow it until it carries us through to making a full circle. In this sacred circle, we find our spiritual center. This center, in turn, is merely a point on the greater circle including other people with their unique paths and ways of being. In joining our different journeys, we all find the greater center connecting us as one.

In this way we each feed and nourish our spiritual way of being, enabling the ancient lessons to be shown to everyone. Perhaps the simplest and most basic truth we will find is that we all face the same challenge of walking the sacred road. In the recognition of this equality, any over-importance of our individuality dies. This death, in turn, enables our emptiness to be filled with identity and connection with everyone. In this movement of emptying and filling, the tides of life's most vital energy will move us, breathe us, and shake us to be alive in the life of all that has lived in the past, all that lives at present, and all that will live in our many futures.

Although my shamanic walk of initiation intersected many traditions, the spirit of the great Oglala Sioux holy man, Black Elk, always was present. This was the case in the beginning, the middle, and the end. Interestingly, Black Elk's own spiritual journey had taken him into both Native American and Christian traditions. I also discovered that he had died at approximately the same time I had been conceived. Because of his presence, I knew the time was coming to go to South Dakota and make a prayer for the old sacred ways. At this time, Ed McGaa, author of the best-selling book on Oglala spirituality, *Mother Earth Spirituality*, reminded me of the words of the great holy man Chief Fools Crow: "These ceremonies do not belong to Indians alone. They can be done by all who have the right attitude — who are honest and sincere about their beliefs in Wakan Tanka (Great Spirit) and follow the rules."

Once, while dancing the Ghost Dance and crying for a return of the old holy ways, Black Elk began to feel an unusual sensation in his body that led him to sway back and forth. He then saw an eagle feather fall before him that turned into a spotted eagle. As if flying with this eagle, he looked down and saw people gathered in a great circle. In the center was a tree in full bloom with flowers. He then knew that if people would live inside the sacred ways, the holy tree would bloom and the sacred circle would be healed. This vision brought forth the same understanding that had come to me after traversing all four directions in my spiritual odyssey.

I knew I must travel to the Black Hills and climb Harney Peak, the place Black Elk's vision indicated was the center of the world. In the latter days of his life, Black Elk climbed to the top of Harney Peak and made a prayer asking that the sacred stick be allowed to bloom. During his prayer, clouds came up and a chill rain fell with the sound of low thunder. My journey of initiation would end at this sacred place in the Black Hills. I would take the sacred stick given to me and make a prayer that the earth and its spiritual ways would bloom.

Before going out to Harney Peak, I reflected on a recent trip to Brazil where I was introduced to a well-respected healer in Sao Paulo. I had been invited to give a speech there and dreamed of seeing a healer who was a heavy set, older, African woman. With only that information, I asked my host, Sylvia, if she could locate the woman in Sao Paulo, one of the largest cities in the world. To our surprise, a friend said she knew a healer fitting the description. A meeting was immediately arranged with Euridice Coelho de Lima.

When we knocked on her front door, the sky began thundering and dropping large hail. This began at the very instant we touched her door, not a second before or after. Euridice said this was the strongest possible sign the spirits could give to bless our meeting. She recognized me as a healer, identified Jesus as my spiritual guide, and told about her participation in leading Umbanda ceremonies. Every year she hosted a great "party" in honor of their spirits. They went to the sea to conduct this ritual. When she placed some beads over my head, the spirit of her "grandfather" spoke. She invited me to return to Brazil to participate in their forthcoming rituals. She wanted me to embody the presence of their healing spirit. At the end of our time together, she gave me many necklaces for protection and celebrated the light she saw surrounding me.

I will never forget the sound of the thunder and the sight of flying hailstones when I visited Euridice. It reminded me of other times in my journey when the thunderbeings came forth. Once in a keynote address at a conference, I challenged the arrogance of the mental health professions and asked for a return to the lessons of humility that come from the ancient traditions. Immediately after that talk, the skies let loose with the forces of thunder. The thunderbeings had sounded many times before whenever I was called to speak on behalf of the ancient sacred ways.

The trip to Harney Peak filled me with a new sense of beginning all over again. I would make a prayer completing a long journey of initiation. I was heading into Black Elk's spiritual homeland, a place where he had held a sacred relationship with the thunderbeings. In that part of the world, he had received a great vision about saving the sacred hoop and the old spiritual ways of his people. Here he shared this vision with John Neihardt so that others could know it. Here a holy seed was planted. The tree of wisdom it brought forth rooted the understanding that saving the old sacred ways was necessary for saving the world. Here I would ask the spirits for guidance. Here my life would begin again, born with the re-newed desire to participate in the evocation of healing, to serve the religion of the Great Mother, and to help bring the different traditions together to pray for the healing of the sacred circle.

On the drive to South Dakota, it rained day and night with severe thunderstorm activity. When I arrived, everything in the Black Hills was covered with fog. It was impossible to see any peak. This weather kept away the tourists and allowed me to approach the sacred site without being disturbed. As I approached the trail toward Harney Peak, the fog lifted. There was no fog around Harney Peak, although it was foggy and raining everywhere else in the area. At the peak of the mountain, I placed the sacred tree into the ground and remembered Black Elk's prayer. I sang and prayed for the healing of the sacred circle. As I held my pipe and aimed it toward the sky, the sun broke through the clouds and stared directly at me. I knew the journey of initiation was complete.

I walked away and at the end of the trail it began to rain again. I looked at the holy stick and noticed that one of the feathers had lost the blue thread formerly gripping its end. I cautiously wondered whether the cleans-ing had begun and whether the old spiritual ways would be saved. At that moment, the words of Black Elk's prayer on top of Harney Peak echoed in my mind: "Grandfather, the Great Spirit, behold us on earth, the two-leggeds. The flowering stick you have given me has not bloomed, and my people are in despair. . . And to the center of the earth you have set a sacred stick that should bloom. . . Oh hear me, grandfathers, and help us, that our generation in the future will live and walk the good road with the flow-ering stick to success. Hear me, and hear our plea."

The cleansing waters of Mother Earth sometimes flow through my own tears. One evening my nine-year-old son had to be rushed to the emergency room because he could barely breathe. The doctors told us he had pneumonia and instructed me to sit by his side all night to monitor his breathing. When he fell asleep, I felt the overwhelming weight of my love and caring for him. The very core of my heart was touched in a way every parent has known when they fully submit to facing how much they love their children.

My tears flowed throughout the night. I wept to voice my love for him. I also wept for the pain I felt because I could not be more present in his life. I wept for the world of suffering he, too, like all other human beings, would necessarily face as he grew up.

During this flow of healing waters, a small miracle took place. The wheezing in his congested lungs turned into a haunting melodic voice. As he slept, the sound of an infant coyote began to fill the room. It was the same music I had heard on the cliff of my first vision fast. That song re-entered my life through the body of my son.

I heard in that song how suffering was a gate to spiritual peace. As the life of Jesus taught us, we must embrace the pain and suffering life brings. Through faith, we spiritually act to transform suffering into a spiritual fire, a fire providing the light leading us to the great, calm, still point. There we find peace through being centered by the sacred circle of healing.

Mother Teresa teaches us to accept everything in life as a gift from God, even when it is sickness or personal ruin. Our responsibility is to act with love toward everyone so that all offerings of life may be transformed into spiritual blessings. Jesus, the shaman who turned water into wine and fed a multitude with a few loaves of bread, left us with the greatest miracle, the miracle of transforming the sufferings of life into the blessings of life through a faith enacted by love.

When I graduated from high school and left home, my mother, a teacher and principal, wrote me a letter, saying, "Although Christ did not promise an easy life, you should never forget to give Him thanks for both the smooth and rough tides in life." She went on to write, "He has no hands but your hands and no feet but your feet with which to achieve His purpose on this earth."

It took me many years to return to the wisdom of her advice. My life had to be broken and a spiritual journey embarked upon that took me to all corners of the earth before I could fully accept what I had grown up hearing as a child in a country church.

Ram Dass, a respected spiritual teacher of our time, also took a pilgrimage that led him to a similar place. Following years as a professor of psychology at Harvard University, he went to India to find his guru. The man he found in India had a blanket, sat on a wooden table, had no possessions, was not interested in having anyone around him all the time, and would often disappear into the jungle. For a period of five months, Ram Dass only saw him three times for around thirty minutes. After a year he came back again to see him. What surprised Ram Dass was that his guru spoke repeatedly about Christ. In his own words (Steindl-Rast, Brother David and Ram Dass, 'On Lay Monasticism,' *The Journal of Transpersonal Psychology*, Volume 9, 1977, pp. 132-133), "I had gone to India, a Jew had gone to a Hindu temple, to be introduced to the New Testament, and when I came to India my guru talked about Christ."

Maharaji said to him, "Christ is your guru . . . He never died. He lives in everyone's heart. Be like Christ . . . Christ told the truth. They killed him for it, but he told the truth. Be like Christ, Christ died for love . . . They slandered Him but it didn't matter." When Maharaji was asked how to meditate like Christ, "he closed his eyes and tears ran down his cheeks and he opened his eyes and said, 'He lost himself into the ocean of love.'" When asked how one can know God, he answered, "Feed everyone." When asked how to awaken Kundalini, he said, "Serve everyone." When asked again how one can know God, he answered, "Love everyone."

The great traditions of shamanism, with their emphasis upon direct communion with the spirit world, teach us that the boundaries imposed by religious institutions and their texts are artificial. Siberian shamans may commune with the Virgin Mary, Native American medicine people may converse with Christ, and Christian shamans may fly with the eagle. There is a sacred circle connecting everything that is holy. Independent of which tradition one enters, the ascents and descents of an impeccable spiritual journey will always lead one to that center point of great stillness. There, the strongest medicine of earth, love, will break our hearts and open our minds to be free of our own self-imposed limitations. There we surrender and die to be reborn to the hope that a meaningful life is made through the action of being a good steward. We truly receive all we need when we give all we have. That is all we need to know.

We live in a time when Mother Earth and her many children are struggling to survive. Our oldest custodians, the ancient cultural healing traditions, face the danger of extinction. Our stewardship must immediately address these traditions and custodians of life. We cannot afford a future without them. We cannot wait any longer to act. We must return home to the calm center of the sacred circle of healing.

In the words of T. S. Eliot, we must become:

> A condition of complete simplicity
> (costing not less than everything)
> And all shall be well . . .

> The future of life requires nothing less.

An Evocation of Mystery

The black snake must re-enter the belly of the body that has Christ-Eagle in its heart. Only in this spiritually whole body can the middle point between good and evil be found. Here one does not indulge in either evil or good. Indulgence is possible only if there exists a "self" available to indulge. Being good or evil implies the presence of such a pursuing agent. The experience of evil or good feeds the realization of the reality of this self. The death of self leads to a complete absence, a place of nothingness. Here there is no entity or identity that can indulge in good or bad.

The loss of self occurs when one is stretched across all sides of spiritual opposites. This crucifixion on the cross of all opposites leads to the death of self and the birth of being, spiritually, in the center of nothingness. To give everything away — property, ideas, longings, and even one's life as one knows it — is to find that there never was a self to begin with. The emptiness of one's core had simply become filled with the litter of concretized ideas. When all that garbage is disposed of, there is no self to be found. The idea of a self was an illusion, believed in because it was assumed all the stuff must have belonged to someone, namely one's self.

The re-birth of being in nothingness makes all spiritual gifts possible. In this middle spot of the cross of opposites, the energy of life and death may move as freely as the leaves blowing with the wind. Here the natural world enters, not the world of decaying garbage. The winged ones, the green ones, the four-leggeds, mountains, streams, and clouds may fill this emptiness. In this way the outer natural world fills the space of one's inner world. Dreams are the guide to this new way of filling the internal emptiness. What one is shown or told in dream must be found in the natural world. When it is found, the outer and the inner become one. In this way our inner ecology unites with the outer ecology making the distinction between the two impossible. When this takes place we move more toward a oneness with the whole natural world. We become all of our relatives. Knowing that the inside is one with the outside enables us to be in the outside with complete awareness. In this way we surrender our limited mind to become a part of a Greater Mind. This Greater Mind constitutes the mind of healing.

In the Gnostic Gospel of Thomas (Pagels, p. 124), Jesus discusses this: "When you make the two one and when you make the inside like the outside and the outside like the inside, and the above like the below, and when you make the male and female one and the same . . . then you will enter (the kingdom)."

Through sacrifice and the death of the unnatural world we empty ourselves of our self. The natural world is then reborn into us through our dreams. In dream time we set forth on journeys to bring the outer into the inner. The passages across this boundary are the passages into shamanic experience and healing. This boundary or crack between the inner and outer world becomes deeper and wider with every crossing until one day the space in the crack has become the whole. This whole space or emptiness that once separated the inner from the outer becomes the complete emptiness that now embraces the whole natural world.

Coming home to the heart of this great, holy emptiness requires our fullest surrender and participation in shaking out the spirits. The spirits are the guides directing us across the inner and outer interfaces. They exist in the midpoints and provide a "medium" for the processes of transformation. The spirits also cross the interfaces and return over and over again to the Center of the Great Circle embodying everything and nothing. We must help them, as they help us, in being shaken out and moved toward the Center of the Great Circle of Healing.

Photographs

Mantaga, Bushman elder, Central Kalahari

Kalahari Bushman healing ceremony

Kalahari Bushmen children

Mantaga's family, Central Kalahari

Bushman rock engraving of leopard, Bophuthatswana

Healing service in South African village

South African traditional village

Marian and author in traditional village, South Africa

New Salem Missionary Baptist Church

New Salem Missionary Baptist Church

The Reverend W.L. Keeney leading baptism in river (c.1938)

Marian in Africa

Mrs. Ikuko Osumi

Mary, Jesus, and Mary Magdelene, painted by Credo Mutwa

Earth Mother and Christ, sculpted by Credo Mutwa

Contemplative Notes
an Appendix

Shaking

The most characteristic shamanic experience for me has always involved "shaking." In my first vision I was shaken. Since that time almost all my shamanic experience has been associated with my body being spontaneously shaken.

"Shaking" in healing has been reported across many cultural groups. The Siberian Tungus term for shaman, "saman," meaning "one who is excited, moved, raised," is noted by Casanowicz (I.M. Casanowicz, "Shamanism of the Natives of Siberia," Washington, D.C., Annual Report of the Smithsonian Institution, 1924) as descriptive of the shaman's shaking.

In 1374, wildly ecstatic dancing in honor of Saint John took place on the lower Rhine and spread through Germany, the Netherlands, and into France. While dancing, the dancers sang and cried out with shaking bodies and saw visions. The clergy rejected what was happening and tried to exorcise demons from the dancers. In the fifteenth century, this epidemic of dancing broke out again.

Shaking ecstasy was also part of the Quakers' experience, who were so named due to the violent trembling early members of their religious sect experienced. The Quakers' own historian notes that their movements were so intense that "on one occasion the house itself seemed to be shaken." Quaker ministers, however, did not encourage this expression. They tried to stop it and would put their shaking members to bed and medicate them.

When Methodism originated in England under Wesley and Whitefield, their services encouraged much shaking by church members. Wesley writes:

> While I was earnestly inviting all men to enter into the Holiest by this new and living way, many of those that heard began to call upon God with strong cries and tears. . . Others exceedingly trembled and quaked. Some were torn with a kind of convulsive motion in every part of their bodies, and that so violently that

often four or five persons could not hold them (in J. Mooney, *The Ghost Dance Religion and Wounded Knee,* New York: Dover, 1973. p. 940).

The Shakers of England moved to New York in 1780 because of persecution for public dancing, shouting, and shaking. Evans, a Shaker, writes of their shaking:

> Sometimes, after sitting a while in silent meditation, they were seized with a mighty trembling. . . They were often exercised with great agitation of body and limbs, shaking, running, and walking the floor, with a variety of other operations and signs swiftly passing and repassing each other like clouds agitated with a mighty wind." In church they would "form a circle around a party of singers, to whose singing they keep time in dance. At times the excitement and fervor of spirit becomes intense, and their bodily evolutions as rapid as those of the dervishes, although still preserving the order of the dance (p. 942, Mooney).

At the New Salem Missionary Baptist Church I found that spiritual experience may be understood in terms of different levels. The first level is activity that serves to "jump start" one's reception of spirit. This may be a convulsive jerk of an arm, shoulder, or head. Or it may be a shout, a sob, trembling, stomping of feet, jumping, or shaking. Here one looks like one was hit with an electrical charge or shot out of a cannon. When the current is running smoothly, more patterned movements may take place. These are usually in tempo with the musical accompaniment of the organ, percussion, and singing of the choir and congregation. This in turn sets the stage for jump-starting one's reception of a more intense spiritual current. Here someone may go into a frenzy, running up and down the aisle or intensely getting the spirit through vocalizations or body movements. If this pushes one over the next edge, an even more intense experience takes place, where the person passes out, experiences a spiritual death, with or without remembrance of what takes place.

I have experienced a variety of body choreographies with respect to "shaking." Sometimes there is a progressive build-up, while, at other times, there is no build up and the very instant I touch someone, I may go into deeper levels. I have never *not* been able to activate this kind of experience. Like a switch, it can be thrown on anywhere and any time and is always shaped by the context in which it takes place.

My shaking takes many different forms including hand, arm, and leg trembling, varieties of head movements, body swaying, vibrating, oscillating, convulsing, jolts, and jumps. My body's vibrational source sometimes comes from the base of my spine. When this is the case, my body typically vibrates in a slow even rhythm and I express the choreographed movement of a snake-like wave form. This pattern is so natural it seems as if it is being done by an outside source. It requires no bodily effort and I can sustain such movements for hours. When the energy comes from my solar plexus, the body vibrations and shaking can be very intense with fast pulses and rhythms. My body may be shaken either vertically or horizontally or back and forth across these dimensions. The source of the movements may also come from my hips, where each side vibrates back and forth shooting pulses of rhythm throughout my body. I am able to choose a spot on my body and have it be the source of starting vibrations for other parts. Or I can take energies, vibrations, and shakes from one part and direct it to another part of my body.

The most powerful work takes place when there is a combination of chanting and singing, together with the body work. This may be further enhanced by closing my eyes and receiving visionary experience. The more sensory channels that work together, the less one's self is in the way and the more intense the experience. At times my observing self dissociates from these processes and observes what is going on without interference. It's like watching another person do the work. At other times my observing completely disappears and I become almost completely unaware of what is going on. Some of the best work takes place when the conscious mind is used as a tool for concentration. It becomes a focusing device to attend to specific visions, sounds, and feelings.

A Healing Session

In a healing session I often begin by touching the person's left shoulder blade area with my right hand and touching their heart area with my left hand. Upon immediate contact I send high levels of vibrations into their back with my right hand and arm. Then my left and right hands pulse back and forth, establishing waves of energy through their body between their shoulder and heart. If the person seems a bit anxious about this work, I don't begin this strongly. I may just touch them with light fluttering hand movements that I will occasionally increase and decrease as an introduction to the work. As they become more comfortable, I move into deeper levels of vibrating. I don't know how I know how to regulate this process. It simply happens.

For some people, intense work is possible with the first touch. I may work on specific areas or the whole body. I will pull and shake whole limbs, send patterns of waves down spines, do arm and hand dances on their backs, vibrate each finger, and move their whole bodies into rapid pulses. I also do a lot of work on people's heads, vibrating, shaking, pulsing, and dancing with them. Sometimes this work feels like playing the keyboard. It is the same way I open up to receive music and allow the fingers to have a life of their own. The movements are often so quick, ever changing and intense that people's minds can't keep up or track it. It is faster than their minds are able to pattern.

When I chant, speak, or sing it is almost always in unknown languages and sounds. The sounds fit the movements, sometimes providing a kind of musical accompaniment to the body dancing. Sometimes the sound moves to a position of authority and aims to instruct the client's body and unconscious. At other times, when I send sounds directly into parts of their bodies, the sound itself is the major healing instrument.

I can choose to be aware of the spirit(s) that use me to do this work. There seems to be no end to the number of spirits that may come through. I believe each client is met with the spirit they need. These spirits include Jesus, ancient Native American medicine people, spirit birds and animals, Asian and African healers and creatures, and other less identifiable sources.

In illustration of the way my healing sessions go, let me describe a particular session with a woman I had worked with before. I began by having her lie down. I then sent vibrations with my hands and arms into her lower back region, with occasional pulses into the base of her spine. My hands subsequently did what felt like stretching the skin surface of her back. This was preparation for stretching her spine with my left hand on the bottom of her neck and my right hand on her lower back. Periodically I worked gently on her head and neck, sending small vibrations into those areas.

As I went into a deeper place, I began to chant and sing. This, in turn, directed me to do specific forms of more intense work. As I would attend to one part of her body, a particular spirit and song would be sent forth. In this case, I worked on other parts of her body through different spirits and songs.

With this woman, most of the spirits were North American medicine spirits, one African Spirit, and several Asian spirits, including a spirit fish from Japan. At certain moments, the singing and body work stopped and I offered what sounded like advice, though in an unidentifiable language.

I sometimes saw in my mind's eye where I was to touch, at other times I observed the spirit working on her, and at still other times I was completely absorbed in the sounds. Toward the end of the session, I sent mantric like sounds into the middle part of her back. A relaxing Asian song with a folk-like melody brought the intensity down to a calm, and then, with a bolt of energy, my hand felt like it ripped something off her spine, as if I were pulling a zipper from the base of her spine to the bottom of her neck, pulling it off and throwing it away. My hands then lightly fluttered over her back, neck, and head, and the session was over.

Spirit

When I tell people about my experience with "spirits," some say it cannot be true. They believe "spirits" are invented or hallucinated by crazy or psychotic perceivers. It does not help to remind them that the great psychologist Carl Jung also decribed personal experiences with ghosts and spirits.

We are now facing a time when the lazy rejection of spiritual reality is becoming more and more questionable. Through the publication of Jung's autobiography, *Memories, Dreams, and Reflections*, and through the popular books of Carlos Castaneda, many readers have been introduced to shamanic realities. More recently, the anthropologist, Edith Turner has described her own experiences of seeing "spirits." She was moved to conclude that spirits are not a matter of metaphor, symbol, or psychology. For her, spirits can be experienced as real, and she refers to anthropologists who lack such experience as suffering from "a kind of religious frigidity."

Whether one believes one is encountering "spirits," "waking dreams," "dreams," or "unconscious imagery," is less relevant than respecting the learning and guidance coming from such experiences. The "realness" of "spirits" is as slippery as the "realness" of any "experience." As Bateson, Von Foerster, Piaget, and many other scholars remind us, the world we know is largely constructed, that is, invented by how we act. What you see (or don't see) tells us about how you act (or don't act). The more intelligent questions have less to do with worrying about what is really real than with creating what should become realized. Of this we can be sure: the world is going straight to ecological hell. We must act to create another world, another reality that serves rather than consumes life. Is it not wise to consider whether the spirits of Mother Earth can become our teachers and guides in moving us toward the light of life?

My own experience of the spiritual world begins with my feeling spiritual energy or vital life force. I refer to this energy as "spirit" or "spirits." It's called "prana" in India, "mana" in Hawaii and Indonesia, "ki" or "seiki" in Japan, "chi" in China, "num," "ngai," "nye," "nzmbi," "megbe," and "voodoo" in Africa, "maxpe" by the Crow, "wakan" by the Dakota, "xupa" by the Hidatsa, "manitou" by the Algonquian, "jojo" by the Australians, "petara" by the Dajak of Indonesia, "tandi" by the Batak of Sumatra, "hasini" by the Malagasy, "baraka" by Sufis, "yesod" by Jewish cabalists, "ruach" by the Hebrews, and "the Holy Spirit" by Christians. I believe these different names refer to the same source of spirit that is open to all, regardless of knowledge, background, color, culture, gender, or religion.

When one receives spirit, whether in the form of a vision, a song, an idea, a dance, or whatever, one is obligated to act. To fail to transform it, is to risk having its energy degenerate into unhealthy forms. Edgar Cayce gave a reading in which he said, ". . . to know, and not to do, becomes sin." (cited in Thomas Sugrue, *The Story of Edgar Cayce*, N.Y: Dell, 1970, p. 268). In another reading (cited in Harmon Hartzel Bro, *A Seer Out of Season: The Life of Edgar Cayce*, N.Y.: Signet, 1990, p. 223), he said that evil was not radically distinct from good, but "evil is just under good, waiting to be lifted." In this perspective, evil is stagnating, untransformed spiritual energy. Good can be made from evil when its energy is transformed. As Cayce suggests:

> One's weaknesses could become one's greatest strengths if the energy were properly engaged. Anger and hostility could become boldness and courage. Stubbornness could become leadership, which endures where others quit. Deception could become true inventiveness. Sensuality could be turned to healing through re-channeling the life force itself (in Bro, pp. 222-223).

After one learns to be open to spirit and its transformation, another lesson must be learned; namely, whenever one is lifted to great spiritual heights, one eventually falls to the ground again. One of the healthiest places to land following an ecstatic spiritual experience is in the territory of the absurd, that is, the land of belly laughs, teasing, silliness, and the ridiculous. Nothing grounds and tunes one better than a laugh that shakes you to your bones. Laughing is a shaking, and sometimes even a convulsing, that cleans and calms one's body and soul.

Following a binge or dose of good frolicking and laughter one is set to rub one's hands together and do some work, whether in the field or office. One can then go into work with a feeling of lightness, a smile, and replayed remembrances of recently known laughter. In this way, one is well pre-pared to work.

The movement from a spiritually high climate to an experience of the absurd, followed by an invitation to work, is beautifully captured by the Huichol shaman, don Jose, following a night of ecstatic ceremony (cited in Steven McFadden, *Profiles in Wisdom: Native Elders Speak About the Earth*, unpublished manuscript, 1991): "Last night we were flying with the gods, but now we're just idiots again. Back to the cornfield!" Humor brings us back to who we are — fools, idiots, and buffoons. Our experience of the gods takes place because we remove our selves to allow the spirits to use us. When we return, the gods leave and our body is again inherited by a spiritual idiot. Once, upon hearing a remark about his prodigious spiritual gifts, Edgar Cayce commented that when he's conscious, he's merely a below average human being. This humility is not an exercise in being modest about our greatness, it is a realization of our being nothing.

The Wild

There may be no greater place to learn about the spirits than in the wild. During the first week that the trees began to blossom one spring, I visited Poverty Point, the ancient Indian ruin in Louisiana where artifacts have been dated back to 1000 B.C. I talked with a ranger about my hypothesis that the central mound there was in the figure of an owl with sacred trees buried under its wings. As our conversation turned to spiritual matters, the ranger's eyes became filled with tears.

We went off together to talk. He said he had grown up as a strong Baptist, but that this place had shaken him up. Working there for ten years, he had found the place filled with an energy that had healed him, his wife, and his children. He spoke with absolute sincerity and simplicity, saying he was ignorant of these things and that he didn't know what it all meant, but that the place had kept his life together.

The simple humility of this man taught me again that we gain every-thing through assuming nothing. I thanked him for opening his heart, and he offered to help me in any way with my future visits to the sacred site. He also said he would open himself to addressing the importance of trees in that area.

I took a group to the "owl mound" and explained to them the traditional importance of praying to all four directions. I shared my vision of the place and one man, Tom, reported hearing an owl while standing on one of the wings. He told a story of taking some adolescent boys out into the wilderness one winter. A coyote had come close to them and played in the snow for about twenty minutes. They all quietly observed. Upon returning from their trip they went to see the movie, *Dances With Wolves*. After the show, they got into the van and drove down the road and were all in a state of silence. They were stunned when, looking at the side of the road they saw a coyote look back at them. Everyone in the van, Tom said, began sobbing. Nothing was said. Everyone knew that what they knew couldn't be spoken.

The wild is one of our greatest healing and teaching resources. As civilization continues to threaten the survival of wilderness, this way of communing with spirit is threatened. Traditional cultures of the world have learned how to heal through those experiences. A loss of this context of healing may very well threaten our abilities to exist as a species.

In the wild, the meaning of any particular piece of action is minimized by the larger, more encompassing dance of interrelatedness performed by all living organisms. Here the whole context of one's experience more easily becomes the focus, rather than the isolated experience. In the wild all participants are more easily realized as small, rather inconsequential players in the whole. The wild, like a sweat, levels one to the ground. If one fully accepts this leveling to insignificance, an abandonment of self takes place and unity with the wild is possible. One accepts one's part in nature and thereby becomes one with nature.

In the wild, being impotent with fear or being outrageously macho are the same. Both ways of being exaggerate and focus on the importance of self. The courage to both act for life as well as accept one's possible immediate death is a more accurate description of how one should fit into nature. Nature is not a stage on which we perform. It is a body of which we are a part. Our hand is not an independent actor performing on the stage of the rest of our body. It is a part of our whole body. Speaking of them as separate is insane. Using our hand as if it were separate from the rest of us is potentially dangerous. To reconcile our relationship with nature requires acting upon the recognition that we are not separate from it. The hand which is us must be reconnected to the body of nature.

Healing

Healing is fundamentally about connecting hands and other parts back to their bodies. It is not about alleviating or curing localized pains and discomforts, although that may be a consequence. Healing, the process of making whole again, is a way of leading people back to contexts which connect them. It should be no surprise that wilderness areas are often the most appropriate locales for healing.

The Cypriot healer, Spyros Sathi (in Kyriacos C. Markides, *The Magus of Strovoles: The Extraordinary World of a Spiritual Healer*, London: Arkana, 1985) proposes that body balance and health require a certain amount of vibration in order for the Holy Spirit to create and optimally maintain the material body. This healthy, vibratory energy is depleted when we create the vibrations of anxiety, depression, stubbornness, jealousy, judgement, anger, hatred, and so forth. With this depletion of energy, we become disconnected and are made vulnerable to disease. Healing is a reconnecting and refilling of life vibrations.

This idea about healing may be most directly enacted by the ancient Japanese tradition of healing called Seiki-Jutsu or the "Art of Vital Life Force." The earliest writing about this vibratory life energy appears in the Chinese text, *Huang-ti Nei Ching Su Wen (The Yellow Emperor's Classic of Internal Medicine)*. It calls this energy "chi," literally "breath." Chi is described as having two complementary and opposing aspects, the yang (masculine) and yin (feminine). The yang aspect is identified with the masculine direction in nature which is regarded as coming from the sky. It thus flows downwards. The yin aspect derives its feminine direction from the heart and flow upwards. Chi energy enters the body roughly two inches below the navel and deep in one's interior at a point called "tan t'ien" (Chinese) or "tanden" (Japanese") which is sometimes referred to as the "stove" or "furnace."

The flow of this life energy through the body is concentrated in specific pathways or meridians. Many ancient techniques of healing, including acupuncture, do-in, shiatsu, and yoga, address ways of facilitating a balanced, well connected flow of energy throughout the body. In the Japanese practice of Seiki-Jutsu, the Seiki healer places a hand on top of the person's head and a knee against their sacrum. Given in a geographically correct place that lines up with the earth's energy, the whole procedure can be done in fifteen minutes. The rationale for this approach is given by the healer Ikuko Osumi: (Ikuko Osumi and Malcolm Ritchie, *The Shamanic*

Healer: The Healing World of Ikuko Osumi and the Traditional Art of Seiki-Jutsu,
Rochester: Healing Arts Press, 1988) as filling people up with the vital life
energy or Seiki they have lost.

In Osumi's healing work, she places her hand on the patient's head and
delivers Seiki with a loud "Kiai" or series of "Kiai." Kiai is described (p.
222) as "a way of concentrating 'ki' or Seiki energy in the lower belly and
then suddenly releasing it often with a loud cry, grunt, or hissing sound."
The description of an actual case of delivering seiki is given by Osumi
(p.43):

> When I felt the time was right I placed my hand on his head,
> and his head and my hand stuck together like magnets. His body
> started to move backwards and forwards and my hand followed
> his movements. When he had received the Seiki he needed, my
> hand came away from his head and his movement became inde-
> pendent of me. I asked him if his movement became independent
> of me. I asked him if his movement was spontaneous and he said
> that it was. "I feel as though I'm floating on the clouds!" he said.

This direct application of life energy to another is the most basic form
of healing. Throughout all cultures of the world, people have found different ways to activate and utilize the flow of life energy to help others be
restored and renewed. A fully developed spiritual life moves with these
flows of energy, striving to have every breath of life be realized as a full
participation in the vibratory movements of spirit.

It follows that all sources of vibration and movement have potential for
healing. The creation of difference and the rhythmic movement across the
border of a difference constitutes a vibration. Any given vibration may
move through other differences creating a flow of vibrations. The major
pathways of such a current move through stations and centers where
focusing, amplifying, and transforming take place. Healing, from this
vantage point, involves creating differences, creating vibrations (movements across the sides of a difference), and opening up currents of vibration.

One of my favorite "reference marks" about healing is the Ellen Burstyn
movie, *Resurrection*. She plays someone who has a life after death experience following an automobile accident. In her recovery, she discovers she
can heal by touching people and loving them. Although she believes in
God, she does not follow the local minister's beliefs about her conduct. She
honestly admits that she heals by simply touching and loving. Since she
doesn't throw out a barrage of scriptures, the minister accuses her of doing

the devil's work. She finds she not only has to leave a structured religious context, but she has to do her healing in secret, unknown even to the one being healed.

For me, love for another without any purposeful glorification of self and without fear of evil constitutes the lens focusing spiritual energy for healing. Love untainted by fear, control, judgement, possession, and expectation is raw, vibratory, life energy, the energy that fills another with life. It transcends ideologies and social structures and is available everywhere. It is not bought, earned, deserved, or achieved, but free for those who sincerely ask.

From this perspective the life energy available for healing is free from being owned (or possessed) by any religion or spiritual practice. Life energy may arise in a classroom, a camping trip, in a concert, play, sporting event, conversation, quiet meditation and sometimes even in a church! It's hard for some religious people to accept that the spirits don't exclusively reside in religious structures. They are free to roam wherever sincere hearts call. It is as possible for the spirits to reside in the music of a jazz saxophonist in a sleezy bar as it is for the spirits to be absent in a high mass at a cathedral.

When religious worship services and sermons get into judgemental trips or displays of piety, the spirits quickly vanish and the church immediately feels like it has lost its soul. At such a time, the most spiritual thing to do may be to ignite a rippling of belly laughs. Then, the holy spirits may decide to return. When the spirits return, they are available to move people. Connection with the flowing currents of spiritual energy connects one more to all of life. In this connection to the great current, river, and ocean of life's vital force, we are healed. Here one is moved, vibrated, and even shaken by the tides of a great ocean of healing.

The Improvisational Nature of Spirituality

Many psychotherapists worry about which school of therapy is best or most true in the same way that others concern themselves with evaluating what is the one and only true religion. The more mature therapist follows his or her own voice, rather than trying to fit the mold of someone else's style (see Bradford P. Keeney, *Improvisational Therapy*, New York: The Guilford Press, 1991). The same holds true for being a healer, medicine person, shaman, or spiritual person. Rolling Thunder, a Native American medicine man, addressed a conference at the Menninger Foundation with similar words: (in Doug Boyd, *Rolling Thunder*, NY: Delta, 1974 p.92):

> I want to warn you not to copy me, but work out your own method. Our people tell us to be original. If you can watch the method, though, and the way I go about it, maybe that would give you some thoughts about what to follow, what it's all about. Then you work out your own substance, your own songs, your own prayers and things to go with it. It's not good to copy.

Similarly, John Fire Lame Deer (in Lame Deer and Richard Erdoes, *Lame Deer: Seeker of Visions*, N.Y.: Simon and Schuster, 1972, p.156) suggested, "Medicine men — the herb healers as well as our holy men — all have their own personal ways of acting according to their visions. The Great Spirit wants people to be different."

Following one's own visions and listening to what the spirits tell you are the main teachings one needs. As was previously mentioned, teachers can only prepare and take you to a context where you may have an opportunity to encounter the spirits. After that, the spirits take over. As John Fire Lame Deer (pp. 155-156) describes this process:

> The "Wicasa Wakan" loves the silence, wrapping it around himself like a blanket — a loud silence with a voice like thunder which tells him of many things. Such a man likes to be in a place where there is no sound but the humming of insects. . . He talks to the plants and they answer him. He listens to the voices of the "Wama Kaskan" — all those who move upon the earth, the animals. He is at one with them. From all living beings something flows into him all the time, and something flows from him.

Communicating with other living beings is not done by elevating other creatures to our level or thinking that they are like us. To ask whether the coyote or eagle really talks is to imply that those creatures have moved toward being like us. I believe it more accurate to say we should move toward being like them. This doesn't mean bringing ourselves "down" to their level. It is more correct to think that our place in the scheme of things is no more and no less than that of any other living creature.

When we attune (or heal) ourselves to our rightful place, we become fully connected and related to all our relatives. Here we are able to commune and learn from all creatures. Doug Boyd (p. 72) writes, "What the life of Rolling Thunder communicates is that when someone identifies himself, not with his self-image or his thinking process but with the flowers, the snow and all manifestations of the life force, he can do things of which Rolling Thunder speaks."

Getting our being to where it belongs requires freeing ourselves from the contrivances and manipulations of abstraction and thought. Naked mind is different from dressed mind and the former enables us to directly encounter the naked minds of all creatures. As Halifax (Joan Halifax, "Shaman's Journey, Buddhist Path," in Gary Doore, *Shaman's Path*, Boston: Shambhala, 1988, p.203) characterizes this, "For the shaman the world of creatures is the uncontrived, the uncooked, the raw: it is the realm where thought does not interfere."

The purpose of the trials and tribulations of spiritual journeys is to help trip one into falling into this raw, naked, natural way of being. Halifax writes (p.204):

> It is not possible to sign up for a weekend course in shamanism and 'get it.' It is not possible to dream it up, pay for it, or study it. In fact, you cannot really seek it; rather, it seeks you. In a similar context, Richard Baker-roshi once said, 'Enlightenment is an accident. Practice makes you accident-prone.' Becoming a shaman is the same thing. Going on vision quests, making offerings, doing the Sun Dance — none of this makes a person a shaman. Going for days and days without food and water in the coldest and harshest of climates — none of this confers shamanhood. Something has to break inside of you; and then that which is discovered within is found to be raw and absolutely naked. It is a mind that some people know who leave no tracks on their way. It is rare, and it is cultivated in the wilderness.

A Conversation on Spiritual Teachers

A: Are some spiritual teachers better than others?

B: Some are better for you and some are better for her and some are better for him and so forth. For every need of a particular seeker, there exists a perfectly designed teacher.

A: But aren't there bad teachers out there?

B: There are bad teachers for you and bad teachers for her and bad teachers for him and so forth. For every need of a particular seeker, there exists an imperfectly designed teacher, or perhaps I should say, there exists a perfectly designed imperfect teacher. They have their lesson to teach, right?

A: Some teachers warn us about other teachers.

B: And they should, as should those other dangerous teachers warn you about the dangers of those you thought were safe teachers.

A: In all seriousness, aren't some of these new age prophets and teachers saying dangerous things?

B: Everyone says something dangerous to someone. You see, I'm talking about suspending your judgement and evaluation of other teachers and students. By the way, each of us is a teacher to someone and a pupil to someone else. And sometimes we change these roles with the other in the very course of a day or even within a conversation.

A: Do questions about the goodness, effectiveness, mastery, or quality of other teachers provide a lesson for the person asking?

B: And for the person who is tempted to answer them.

A: Traditional Native Indian medicine people are often critical of one another. Some will criticize others who talk about what they do in public.

B: They help keep each other in balance that way. For everyone who goes public about the spiritual world, someone will be quiet.

A: And someone else will talk about both of them.

B: Yes, perhaps you. Let me ask you a question. If you woke up hearing the most beautiful song would you want to write down the music and play it for others?

A: Absolutely. Music that fills our hearts should be shared.

B: Where did that music come from?

A: Music comes from our hearts and souls. Some of the master composers, like Bach, seemed to be a direct channel with a divine source of music. He wrote it down as fast as he heard it.

B: Do you think receiving music is any different than receiving other spiritual gifts?

A: I don't know. Perhaps it is the most spiritual gift of them all. Peruvian shamans are not able to commune with the spirit world with the sacred vine alone. It takes a song to orchestrate and navigate the visions.

B: Do the greatest of composers believe they wrote the music, or do they believe they were the servants of the gods?

A: From what I know, many of them saw themselves as the instrument hooked up to receive and record the music. The music was played through them. Their responsibility was to then give it away to the world.

B: What the world did with it wasn't their responsibility. It might be used as a courtship song, advertisment jingle, elevator music, or an evocation for bringing forth the gods in a great concert hall or cathedral. The music was free to go wherever it happened to go.

A: Are you suggesting that, in general, the great visions and revelations of spiritual people should be released into the world?

B: Have not the greatest visions already been given away? Whether in the Bible, Koran, or in the transcribed words of Black Elk, many of the world's great visions have been opened for the view of all people.

A: Shouldn't one be responsible for the spiritual gifts given one?

B: Isn't one responsibility to set the gift free? If you did not dream it, but were given it, how are you to say you own it?

A: I have heard that the power of a vision is lost when it is given to others.

B: But that frees the dreamer to receive another dream, and another, and another. If you give a gift away, you may lose it, but stand ready to receive another. If you're fixated on holding onto one gift, you may never notice the gifts that await around you.

A: What is the value of being warned about giving our spiritual gifts away?

B: We are reminded of the specialness of these gifts. They are not to be cheaply thrown away, but are to be carefully wrapped and lovingly presented to those who may benefit from them.

A: How about those medicine men who never share any of their visions?

B: They give us the gift of disciplined silence. That is the gift they choose to bestow upon us.

A: Will they understand our giving our visions away?

B: We will be giving them a gift strengthening their desire and discipline to remain silent.

Afterword

When I completed writing this account of my shamanic experiences, I felt drawn to send the manuscript to a particular publisher in New York. Within a week the book was accepted for publication. The publisher and I instantly became joined together in our dedication to the Great Circle of Healing that connects diverse cultural healing traditions. It is extremely rare in the business driven world of publishing to find the kind of spiritual understanding and warm partnership I have found with Station Hill Press. I write these statements because they, too, have become part of the story.

No one can stop the voices of the elders and spirits from being heard. The curtain has opened and light is shining upon the whole of Mother Earth. Our home will be cleansed either by the tears of our suffering and joy or by the floods of sacred waters. The protests and name calling of the diminishing intolerants do not have to be granted any more solidity than the air their voices disturb. We must all keep focused on the illumination of timeless wisdom with its radiance of love, humility, and great healing.

The stories I have shared with you are all true. In closing there are several more stories about the power of the Great Spirit that must be told.

After returning from the rain forests of Paraguay, I once forgot to carry the protection given to me by the Guarani Indians. My vehicle soon was totalled in a collision with a blue car called a Dodge "Spirit." I couldn't help but remember Black Elk's warning about the harm caused by the "blue man." After the accident I attached the feathers of protection to my car. Within several weeks another car slammed into the rear of my car with as great a force as the previous accident. My son and I got out of the car to assess the damage and to our great surprise not a dent or scratch could be found. We have not removed the feathers from the car.

Many doors are opening and connecting people who have experienced the urgency of our present local and global situation. As I speak to conferences and groups of people about the mysteries of the ancient healing traditions, I find more and more light in the human community. There is great hunger for rebecoming our natural way of being.

On the evening of December 12, 1993, I again felt overwhelmed by the burden associated with knowing what the spirits have revealed. I also feared the consequences this book would have on my family life. In a moment of desperation I cried out to the Creator, "I'm not sure I can live with this responsibility. I am doing what you have asked. You must help me endure and show you are with us." In an instant my wife, Marian, and I saw a particular sacred object sitting on a dresser. I had never removed it from my medicine bundle. We began weeping over the shock of its appearance. In the next moment I began to doubt that it had happened, wondering whether someone had done this to us by trickery. In that second of doubt a tiny black clay pot appeared next to the other sacred object. It had been given to me by my Grandfather when I was a child. He had taken me to New Mexico and introduced me to the first Native American I had ever seen. We went to San Ildefonso Pueblo and met Maria Martinez. There he allowed me to choose any pot I wanted. I chose the smallest one. This was the pot that appeared before us.

When we saw the pot we wept again. I cried out to the Great Spirit, "Please stop. You do not have to show us any more. I am completely yours. I will not hold back. Tell us what we are to do."

I know, without a doubt, that miracles take place and that the world is filled with great mysteries. I invite you to abandon any fear of the light and begin a life celebrating the bringing forth of the Great Spirit into all that we may become.

About the Author

Bradford Keeney, Ph.D., is presently Professor, Graduate Programs in Professional Psychology, University of St. Thomas, St. Paul, Minnesota. Internationally renowned for his contributions to systemic thinking and practice, he is the former director of several clinical graduate programs and has worked at the Ackerman Institute for Family Therapy in New York City, the Philadelphia Child Guidance Clinic, and the Menninger Foundation. A fellow of the American Association for Marriage and Family Therapy, he is the author of numerous professional books, including the critically acclaimed *Aesthetics of Change* and *Improvisational Therapy*. He is also a pianist, composer, and author of the forthcoming *The Lunatic Guide to the Late Show with David Letterman* and the children's book *Funny Medicines for Children*.

Further Acknowledgements

Printer's Ornaments

The printer's ornaments in the book are based upon petroglyphs, woodcuts, and drawings from various native cultures. Grateful acknowledgement is due to the following sources for calling these images to our attention and for permission to use them here:

Ornaments on the cover and on pages, 1, 18, 33, 42, 44, 46, 50, 65, 74, 77, 79, 81, 87, 90, 92, 108 are from *Images of Power: Understanding Bushman Art*, David Lewis-Williams and Thomas Dowson, Southern Book Publishers. : Johannesburg, 1989.

Ornaments on pages 8, 10, 14 (drawing after Wellman), 21 (drawing after Campbell Grant), 24 (from *Asia XXIX No. 4*, 1929), 111 (drawing after Wellman), 120, 123, 135 are from *The Wounded Healer*, Joan Halifax, Thames & Hudson Ltd.: London, 1982.

Ornaments on pages 27, 62 are from *Indaba My Children*, Vusamazulu Credo Mutwa, Humanities Press.: 1971.

Ornaments on pages 36, 55 are from *Sun Circles and Human Hands: The Southeastern Indian Art and Industries*, edited by Emma Lila Fundaburk and May Douglas Fundaburk Foreman, Emma Lila Fundaburk Luverne.: Alabama, 1957.

Ornaments on pages 39, 69, 72, 127 are from *Teachings from the American Earth*, edited by Dennis Tedlock and Barbara Tedlock, Liveright.: New York, 1975.

Ornaments on pages 48, 150, 155 are from *Le Bestiaire du Christ*, Louis Charbonneau-Lassay, Desclée, De Brouwer & Cie.: France, 1940.

Ornament on page 70 is from *Supplement to the South African Journal of Science*, special issue no. 2, May, 1971.

Ornament on page 98 is from *The Mystic Spiral*, Jill Purce, Avon.: New York, 1974.

Ornament on page 163 (by Zen Master Sengai, 18th Century) is from *Zen: Direct Pointing to Reality*, edited by Anne Bancroft, Thames and Hudson. : New York, 1979.

Photographic Credits

Back cover photograph by Eduardo Newark, M.D.

Photographs on pages 10, 112 (top), 112 (bottom), 113 (top), 113 (bottom), 164D (top), 164I (top-left), 164I (top-middle), 164I (top-right), 164I (bottom) by Derek Shirley.

Photograph on page 153 courtesy of the National Park Service at Pipestone National Monument.

Photographs on pages 28, 93, 103 (top), 103 (bottom), 107, 164B (top), 164B (bottom), 164C (top), 164C (bottom), 164D (bottom), 164E (top), 164E (bottom), 164G (bottom) by Peter Johnson.

Photographs on pages 30, 51, 147 by the Author.

Photographs on pages 3, 5, 7 by Fernando Fernandez-Andez.

Photographs on pages 136, 143, 164H by Edward Matsuo.

Photograph on page 76 by Diane Meili.

Composite graphic on page 180 by Joanne Tolkoff of photographs "Home in the Kalahari" by Peter Johnson and "Ave Tape Miri, Guarani 'Priest of the Forest'" by Fernando Fernandez Andes.

Grateful acknowledgement is due to Harcourt Brace Jovanovich Inc. for permission to quote from T.S. Eliot's poem, *Four Quartets* from *The Complete Poems and Plays*, © 1962.

A Request for Help

Indigenous healers from around the world are trying to meet one another. They need our financial help to make this possible. If you are willing and able to make a tax-deductible contribution for this purpose to The Sacred Circle Project, please contact:

Institute for Publishing Arts, Inc.
The Sacred Circle Project
Barrytown, New York 12507

Catalogue of Related Titles
from
Station Hill Press

The Shaman's Doorway

Opening Imagination to Power and Myth

STEPHEN LARSEN

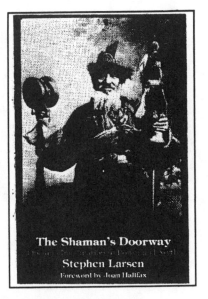

The Shaman's Doorway

Stephen Larsen

Foreword by Joan Halifax

Expanded from the 1976 classic, *The Shaman's Doorway* is the first book to view traditional shamanism from a distinctly modern, psychological perspective. It lends a new understanding to the "inner journey" of our own time. Building on the works of Carl Jung and Joseph Campbell, Larsen offers readers a methodology for traveling through "stages of mythic engagement" — the encounter with spiritual power, death and rebirth, and the gaining of mystical vision—leading to the highest level of dialogue with the imagination: the way of the creative artist, the visionary warrior, and the modern shaman.

Stephen Larsen, authorized biographer of Joseph Campbell, is a pyschotherapist, teacher, and author of *The Mythic Imagination*.

$10.95 paper, ISBN 0-88268-072-2, 6 x 9, 260 pages, 25 photos of shamanistic materials, notes, bibliography, index.

Sam Woods
American Healing
STAN RUSHWORTH

This unusual and eloquent book is not about healing technique, but is an extraordinary exploration into the healing spirit. Weaving together prayers and stories, Sam Woods reveals a fascinating world of healings, revelation and discovery through healing, and attitudes toward healing; the book becomes a healing unto itself as we begin to feel and see the way Sam Woods moves through his life. With prayer and praise, illumination and judgment, a healer's view of living today is opened to us, and we see how we are drawn to fall away from the Earth, and how we come back.

Sam Woods says, "This book is a joining, a listening to the voices of the earth, of the hawk and frog, of the children, of the people. It is a long prayer, a gathering together, a quiet walk into seeing, carrying everything with us as we go, our history, our ancestors, our sorrow, and our promise."

$11.95 paper, ISBN 0-88268-122-2, 5 1/2 x 8 1/2, 292 pages.

Screaming Hawk
The Training of a Mystic Warrior
PATTON BOYLE

This visionary narrative, reminiscent of Richard Bach's *Illusions*, follows the spiritual initiation of a white Christian into the Native American tradition and reveals a deeper Christian impulse that is consistent with Native American wisdom. Set in the western United States on an unnamed Indian reservation, the novel describes the seeker, a White Man who has come to the home of Native American medicine man, Flying Eagle. Through Flying Eagle's teachings on a variety of subjects, the protagonist awakens to a new understanding of self, the nature of truth, and the role of a warrior for truth. With reverberations of Carlos Castaneda, *Screaming Hawk* becomes not just a novel of traditional and Native American religion, but also a compelling spiritual journey for its readers.

Patton Boyle, an Episcopal minister and psychological counselor, lives in Corvallis, Oregon.

$9.95, ISBN 0-88268-159-1, 6 x 9, 136 pages.

A Journey to the Ancestral Self

The Native Lifeway Guide to Living in Harmony with Earth Mother

TAMARACK SONG

"For the deer and the grasses I have written this book, so that we may again be At One with them." Thus writes Tamarack Song, in this extraordinary, practical guide to native lifeways — the essential wisdom connecting all native peoples. Though the author is white, the book speaks to readers from every background who seek a connection with their essential self — that person, deep within each of us, "who dances to the Drum around the ritual Fire, who knows healing lore from times when plants spoke, who yearns for the peace and Blessings of walking again in the Balance of Our Earth." In clear but evocative language, the author shares his unique message: that the lifeways of all Native peoples are essentially one, sharing not just the same ceremonies and life transitions, but the same spirit and reverence for life; and that all of us, regardless of ethnic background or religious upbringing, are essentially Native people. The book begins by demonstrating how native lifeways— the ways of the Guardian Warrior, the caretaking of children, reverence for elders ("Keeping the Ancestral Voice"), and many more — are intrinsic to the human experience. Drawing on a series of native traditions — from fasting and feasting to dreams and the receiving of visions — the book then shows the reader how to bring to life those intuitive, sensory, and spiritual powers that have been long-hidden and little used.

Tamarack Song founded Teaching Drum School to pass along native lifeways in a wilderness setting. He lives in Three Lakes, Wisconsin.

$14.95 paper, ISBN 0-88268-178-8, 6 x 9, 264 pages, 11 graphs, 20 drawings, bibliography, index.

Gently Whispered

*Oral Teachings by
the Very Venerable
Kalu Rinpoche*

Foreword by H.E. the XIIth Tai Situpa

This compilation of teachings presents the oral wisdom of Kalu Rinpoche, revered worldwide as a teacher of Vajrayana Buddhism. Here are his views on the mastery of the three *yanas,* the vows of Refuge and Bodhisattva, and the true nature of the mind. Also included are techniques for stepping beyond the Four Veils of Obscuration and Emotional Subjectivity onto the Five Paths that culminate in the liberation of *mahamadra,* plus a thorough introduction to the visualization techniques of *yidam* practice, a detailed commentary on the *Chenrezig sadhana,* and an extensive explanation of the Bardos of Death and Dying. Leavened with humor and fresh insight, this first English translation is an excellent resource for the novice and experienced student alike.

Kalu Rinpoche (d. 1989), a celebrated teacher of Tibetan Buddhism, was the head of the Shangpa Kagyu lineage and founder of numerous Kalu Rinpoche centers around the world.

$15.95 paper, ISBN 0-88268-153-2, 6 x 9, 304 pages.

Wonders of the Natural Mind

*The Essence of Dzogchen in
the Bon Tradition of Tibet*

TENZIN WANGYAL

Foreword by Lopon Tenzin Namdak

The Bon are the indigenous, pre-Buddhist natives of Tibet, and *Wonders of the Natural Mind* is the first introduction to the popular Dzogchen philosophy from the Bon perspective, fully compatible with the major Buddhist teachings. For the growing number of Westerners interested in Dzogchen, Wangyal explains the specific meaning of the teachings, and takes the reader step by step through their practice. He covers both meditation and the visionary aspects of Dzogchen previously regarded as secret.

Tenzin Wangyal is a *geshe* (the Tibetan equivalent of professor) with many years of experience under Lopon Tenzin Namdak, head of the Bon lineage. Formally trained in India, Nepal, and Norway, Wangyal has set up a teaching institute in Charlotteville, Virginia, and is presently at Rice University in Houston under a Rockefeller Fellowship.

$14.95 paper, ISBN 0-88268-117-6, 6 x 9, 256 pages.

Self-Liberation Through Seeing With Naked Awareness

An Introduction to the Nature of One's Own Mind in the Tibetan Dzogchen Tradition

Translated and edited, with introduction and commentary
by John Reynolds
Foreword by Namkhai Norbu

This is the first authentic translation of *The Tibetan Book of the Great Liberation*, a fundamental classic on personal transformation that is derived from the same "treasure text" as the *Tibetan Book of the Dead*. Once poorly translated by Evans-Wentz, this new version by a celebrated Tibetologist reveals clearly what is said in the original text. The nature of Dzogchen, not a philosophy or sect but the primordial state of every individual, transcending intellectual and cultural limitations, is discussed at length in John Reynolds' extensive commentary, based on the oral teachings of Namkhai Norbu Rinpoche, Lama Tarchen Rinpoche, and his Holiness Dudjom Rinpoche.

$29.95 cloth, ISBN 0-88268-058-7, 6 x 9, 240 pages. Order No. P0501, $14.95 paper ISBN 0-88268-050-1

The Cycle of Day and Night

An Essential Tibetan Text on the Practice of Contemplation

NAMKHAI NORBU

Translated by John Myrdhin Reynolds

Namkhai Norbu clearly presents the ancient tradition and includes instruction in contemplative practices that are integrated with activities in both waking and sleeping states. Based on a teaching by Garab Dorje, the first human master of the Dzogchen lineage, this book gives a translation of the author's Tibetan text, together with a commentary drawn from his oral explanations.

Namkhai Norbu Rinpoche is a Tibetan Lama who, from 1964 until the present, has been a professor of the Oriental Institute of the University of Naples, Italy, where he teaches Tibetan and Mongolian languages and Tibetan cultural history.

$10.95 paper, ISBN 0-88268-040-4, 5½ x 8½, 128 pages.

Thunder's Grace

MARY ELIZABETH THUNDER

WALKING THE ROAD OF VISIONS
WITH MY LAKOTA GRANDMOTHER

MARY ELIZABETH THUNDER

A part-Indian woman who was searching for her roots found much more . . . acceptance of a Mother. Abandoned by her real mother when she was three weeks old, Mary Elizabeth Thunder survived abuse, a broken marriage, and a death experience during an operation after a heart attack to become a self-actualized woman leader and teacher. The late Grace Spotted Eagle, who asked Thunder to write this book for all women to know no matter how hard their life has been, they too can have a life that is full of love, laughter, and joy working itself out of the dysfunction perimeters through ceremonies. Thunder's story is the true tale of a remarkable elder, Grandma Grace Spotted Eagle, who adopted her and guided her in a spiritual awakening as a messenger. At once harrowing and uplifting, this memoir takes us from Thunder's early life and experiences with legendary elders such as Grace Spotted Eagle, Wallace Black Elk, Rolling Thunder, and Chief Leonard Crow Dog, through the death experience that utterly transformed her, to over nine remarkable years she spent traveling America by van, culminating in her inclusion in the Sun Dance, one of the world's oldest and most venerable initiations on the North American Continent. Intimate, painfully honest, essentially and overwhelmingly spiritual, this is a book about a woman's quest for meaning amid two cultures and a compelling account of the visionary side of Native American life.

Mary Elizabeth Thunder, is a well known Speaker, Human Rights Advocate, Sundancer, Peace Elder, Mother, Grandmother, and Wife of Native and Non-Native descent. She has traveled globally now to share a message of Peace and healing of the earth by healing of oneself. She and her husband Jeffery Hubbell live and maintain a ranch which is a Spiritual University in West Point, Texas.

$14.95p, ISBN 0-88268-166-4, 256 pages, 40 b&w photos.

Death is of Vital Importance
On Life, Death, and Life After Death
ELISABETH KÜBLER-ROSS, M.D.

Five intimate, conversational talks, edited from speaking engagements, offer an overview of the life and work of a woman who has been as influential as she is remarkable. Enlivened with dozens of striking case histories and memorable stories from the author's own childhood, the book recounts such events as her extraordinary meeting with a woman in the German concentration camp of Maidanek a few months after the war, here mother's death, and her own near-death experience and epiphany of "cosmic consciousness." Also included is a step-by-step breakdown of the experience of dying, descriptions of the differences among physical, psychic, and spiritual energy and of her method for interpreting children's drawings, based on Jung's theory (and later expanded by Dr. Bernie Siegel). She offers insights into the now-famous story of Dougy, the young boy whose question "Why do little children have to die?" led her to create the best-selling Dougy Letter, and proposed the establishment of ET (elderly-toddler) centers, where children can be "spoiled rotten." At the end of this special book, readers will feel that they have spent a privileged evening in the presence of a wonderful and very wise woman.

Elizabeth Kübler-Ross, author of the international bestseller *On Death and Dying*, has been one of the most prominent pioneers of the hospice movement. Her farm near Staunton, Virginia, is also a retreat and workshop center.

$12.95p, ISBN 0-88268-186-9; 216 pages, 6 x 9, bibliography.